Technical Analysis Simplified

By Clif Droke

Marketplace Books
Columbia, MD

Contents

Introduction

*"The principles of successful stock speculation are based
on the supposition that people will continue in the future to
make the mistakes that they have made in the past."*
— Reminiscences of a Stock Operator

It is no exaggeration to say that technical analysis of equity
and commodity trends affords one of the greatest hopes of
achieving the ultimate end of free enterprise-profit. In fact,
without the use of this peerless tool, most investors will find
themselves at the mercy and whim of market forces beyond
their comprehension. In sum, technical analysis is the best
means possible for attaining financial profit and for understanding the underlying condition of the economy as well as
general societal trends.

By simplified technical analysis we mean a combination, a
dynamic symmetry if you will, of various forms of technical
chart pattern analysis that combines the simplest and most
basic elements of this discipline with a useful admixture of
proven, more modern methods of technical analysis. This mixture of various forms of technical analysis will, if integrated
properly, provide a powerful tool for predicting the future
course of the markets being analyzed. The overriding goal of
our simplified technical analysis is an easy-to-use, highly effective combination of proven analytical techniques from both
classical and modern forms of technical analysis.

And just what is that optimal mixture? While we do not pretend to know beyond all doubt, we have arrived-through careful research and practical application-at that combination of
forms we feel most effective. It is within the pages that follow
that we intend to explain our findings in a way that will allow
the reader to apply them for himself and profit thereby.

Chapter 1

What is Technical Analysis?

The stock market or any market never reflects what its true value is. It reflects investors' perception of the value of what people think it is worth.

The price of any given security does not measure current conditions of supply and demand, but future expectations of supply and demand.

What is technical analysis? Many observers look upon technical analysis as a collection of gimmicks and of more or less serious practices. Indeed, practitioners of the discipline are often characterized as "witch doctors." Still others acknowledge its validity but question its accuracy in forecasting important trends in the stock and commodity markets. Among practitioners of technical analysis (and while it can be neither purely described as "art" or "science," but sharing elements of both, so that we will call it a "scientific art") there exists no uniform consensus as to what it constitutes.

Broadly defined, it is an attempt at understanding the current state or health of a market or individual equity or commodity (referred to hereafter as a "security") with a goal towards forecasting future price movement by relying on historical market (or chart) patterns. The underlying assumption in technical analysis is that a firm knowledge of past price/chart pattern behavior will confer insight as to where prices are heading in the near future as well as to what can be expected in a particular market.

Perhaps it will help to see how others have defined it. Drs. Nick and Barbara Apostolou define it as a "process of predicting future stock price movements by analyzing the historical movement of stock prices and supply and demand forces that affect those prices." [1] The Apostolous, however, seem to equate technical analysis, at least in some part, with fundamental analysis (which is the process of estimating the value of a security or commodity by analyzing the basic financial and economic conditions of the person(s), companies, or industry sectors behind the securities).

Norman G. Fosback, in his classic best-selling book, *Stock Market Logic*, has this to say of the competing methods:

"While the essence of fundamental analysis is the determination of value and the purchase or sale of stocks whose price deviates from value, technical analysis is based upon two very different premises. First, that subjective estimates of value are simply too imprecise and are thus effectively irrelevant. Second, that future price fluctuations may be predicted through analyses of historical price movements, supply and demand relationships, and other factors which impact directly upon price." [2]

Clifford Pistolese's definition is lucid as it is comprehensive:

"[Technical analysis is] the use of price and volume charts as the basis for investment decisions. The rationale for this approach is that the price and volume information in the chart reflects all that is known about the company by all the interested parties who have bought or sold that stock. Since

*the stock chart summarizes and displays the net result of all
these buy and sell decisions, it is the best single resource for
making rational investment decisions."[3]*

R.W. Schabacker, the grandfather of modern technical analysis, aptly describes technical chart analysis as "the New
Science."[4] He demonstrates that all relevant fundamental factors
are "brought to bear, are evaluated and automatically weighted
and recorded in net balance on the stock chart."[5] He further
characterizes the stock or commodity chart as "the complete
memory" of the market and postulates that "the stock chart's
chief value therefore grows out of its being a pictorial record of
trading history."[6] He defines technical analysis as:

*"Technical market action is that aspect of analysis which is
based upon phenomena arising out of the market itself, to
the exclusion of fundamental and all other factors. In fact,
technical action may also be explained as merely the antithesis of the fundamental considerations. The fundamental
aspect of market analysis lays special stress upon such factors
as the corporation behind the stock, its business, its prospects,
its past, present and future earnings, its balance sheet, its
financial strength, the quality of its management and so
on...The technical factors are what might be termed the resid-
ium of the total sum of all aspects bearing upon their probable market value of the stock, after the more apparent and
fundamental factors are eliminated."[7]*

Our survey of the definitions of technical analysis by various
commentators would by no means be complete without the
insight provided by the venerable Robert D. Edwards and John
Magee, who draw distinction to the term "technical" itself by
pronouncing it "the study of the action of the market itself as
opposed to the study of the goods in which the market deals."[8]
For a working definition of technical analysis, they state:

*"Technical analysis is the science of recording, usually in
graphic form, the actual history of trading (price changes,
volume of transactions, etc.) in a certain stock or in 'the aver-*

ages' and then deducing from that pictured history the probable future trend." [9]

Further embellishing their definition they state:

"...the technician claims with complete justification, that the bulk of the statistics which the fundamentalists study are past history, already out of date and sterile, because the market is not interested in the past or even in the present! It is constantly looking ahead; attempting to discount future developments, weighing and balancing all the estimates and guesses of hundreds of investors who look into the future from different points of view and through glasses of many hues. In brief, the going price, as established by the market itself, comprehends all the fundamental information which the statistical analyst can hope to learn (plus some which is perhaps secret from him, known only to a few insiders) and much else besides of equal or even greater importance. [10]

Edwards & Magee provide further elucidation on this subject by listing four basic points which give meaning and value to technical analysis. The points are as follows:

- The market value of a security is determined solely by the interaction of supply and demand.
- Supply and demand are governed at any given moment by many hundreds of factors, some rational and some irrational. Information, opinions, moods, guesses (shrewd or otherwise) as to the future, combine and blend necessities into this equation. No ordinary man can hope to grasp and weigh them all, but the market does this automatically.
- Disregarding minor fluctuations, prices move in trends which persist for an appreciable length of time.
- Changes in trend, which represent an important shift in the balance between supply and demand, however caused, are detectable sooner or later in the action of the market itself. [11]

Finally, we include Steven B. Achelis' definition of technical analysis, which he asserts is "the study of prices, with charts being the primary tool, to make better investments." [12] He continues:

The roots of modern-day technical analysis stem from the Dow Theory, developed around 1900 by Charles Dow. Stemming either directly or indirectly from the Dow Theory, these roots include such principles as the trending nature of prices, prices discounting all known information, confirmation and divergence, volume mirroring changes in price, and support/resistance. And of course, the widely followed Dow Jones Industrial Average is a direct offspring of the Dow Theory. Charles Dow's contribution to modern day technical analysis cannot be understated. His focus on the basics of security price movement gave rise to a completely new method of analyzing the markets." [13]

Thus, it is only fitting that we begin our examination of technical analysis with the famous Dow Theory.

Notes

[1] Apostolou, Nick and Barbara, *Keys to Investing in Common Stocks,* Barron's, 1995, pg. 136

[2] Fosback, Norman G., *Stock Market Logic,* Dearborn Financial Publishing, 1976, 1993, pg. 198

[3] Schabacker, R.W., *Technical Analysis and Stock Market*

Profits, Pitman Publishing, 1997
(originally published in 1932), pg. 6

[4] Ibid., pg. 4

[5] Ibid., pg. 6

[6] Ibid., pgs. 6-7

[7] Edwards & Magee, *Technical Analysis of Stock Trends,*
Amacom, 1948, 1997, pg. 4

[8] Ibid., pg. 4

[9] Ibid., pg. 4

[10] Ibid., pgs. 6-7

[11] Ibid., pg. 106

[12] Achelis, Steven B., *Technical Analysis From A to Z,* Irwin,
1995, pg. 2

[13] Ibid., pg. 2

Chapter 2

The Dow Theory

Much lip service is paid to the famous Dow Theory by today's investors. Yet comparatively few are familiar with its basic tenets. Even fewer actually incorporate the tenets of the Dow Theory into their day-to-day trading regimes or investment strategies. Our first task, therefore, is to dispel this ignorance and explain as lucidly and concisely as possible what those tenets are. But this is no difficult task as the Dow Theory is of all theories of stock market analysis the simplest and easiest to understand. That's because the theory's progenitor, long-time *Wall Street Journal* editor Charles Dow, would have it no other way.

While viewed as archaic and anachronistic by many, the Dow Theory is the grandfather of all theories of technical analysis-the foundation, if you will-of our very craft as market technicians. Furthermore, we find that its reliability is unchanged even today in a much more complex marketplace than Dow himself dealt with. In short, it has survived the test of time and is the prototype from which all other theories of technical analysis derive. An understanding of Dow Theory, therefore, is crucial to our examination of the subject of technical analysis. The Dow Theory must be the base from which all further endeavor in technical analysis is laid.

Before we can comprehend Dow's Theory, however, we must first understand a little of Charles Dow himself. To do this we turn to one of the early authorities on Dow Theory and an original Dow chronicler-Robert Rhea, from his classic work, *The Dow Theory.* Rhea writes:

"Charles H. Dow, founder of the country's greatest financial news agency—Dow, Jones & Company—was one of the owners of The Wall Street Journal, which he edited until his death in 1902. During the last few years of his life he wrote a few editorials dealing with stock speculation which are the only personal record we have of his observations of recurring characteristics of the stock market. These observations were based upon the movement of daily average prices of railroad and industrial stocks included in the Dow-Jones Averages.

"Mr. Dow did not designate his stock market observations as the Dow Theory. That was done by his friend S.A. Nelson, who wrote The ABC of Stock Speculation in 1902. It was he who first attempted to explain Dow's methods in a practical manner.

"Many successful men today believe the implications of the daily movement of the Dow-Jones rail and industrial averages to be the most dependable indicator of both price and business trends yet devised, and they usually refer to inferences drawn from the movement of the averages as the 'Dow Theory.'

"Until 1897 only one stock average had been kept by Dow, Jones & Co., but at the beginning of that year separate averages were started for railroad and industrial stocks. During the time Dow wrote, he had at the most only a five-year record of both averages to examine, and it is indeed remarkable that he was able, in so short a time, to establish the fundamentals of such a useful theory of price movement based on the dual averages. It is true that some of his conclusions later proved to be erroneous, but the fundamentals have

proved sound when tested against market movements for 28 years after his death. [1]

"William Peter Hamilton, who served under Dow, carried on the study and interpretation of the theory through occasional editorial forecasts. His observations and predictions generally proved to be accurate, with the result that they soon became one of the most popular features of The Wall Street Journal until his death in December 1929.

"In 1922 Hamilton wrote The Stock Market Barometer, a book in which he explained the Dow Theory in more detail than was possible within the limitations of editorial comment. This book achieved a genuine success... It provoked a veritable storm of controversy, repercussions of which may yet be occasionally noticed in financial columns. One of the primary reasons for this controversy is the general unwillingness of those who claim ability to forecast stock market trends by means of elaborate statistical research to concede the usefulness of the Dow Theory. These critics are usually entirely ignorant of the principles underlying this valuable and workable theory.

"The development of the automobile and of the Dow Theory since 1902 have certain similarities. To the automobile of 1902, our engineers later added improved motor power, demountable rims, electric lights, self-starters, and other needed refinements which eventually gave us a reliable and convenient means of transportation. In a similar manner, Hamilton tested and improved the Dow Theory between 1902 and 1929. As the record of the averages unfolded with the years, he gave us a well-defined and exceptionally reliable method of forecasting the trends of both stock prices and business activity.

"It is no great job to put together a mass of figures derived from past business records and make an index which is supposed to forecast trends reliably. The trouble with all such

methods is that they deal with the past and, of necessity, must, to a great extent, be based on the assumption that history will repeat itself. Then, before the value of such an index can be accepted, it must be tested for a great many years against actual developments. Dow's theory has survived just such a test." [2]

In order to understand how completely Hamilton believed the stock averages were effective as forecasting mediums, a number of selections from his editorials over a 25-year period (excerpted by Rhea) are quoted below:

"Study of the averages is based on Dow's theory, propounded by the late Charles H. Dow, the founder of [The Wall Street Journal]. The books which published that theory seem to be out of print, but briefly it was this: Simultaneously in any broad stock market there are—acting, reacting and interacting—three definite movements. That on the surface is the daily fluctuation; the second is a briefer movement typified by the reaction in a bull market or the sharp recovery in a bear market which has been oversold; the third and main movement is that which decides the trend over a period of many months, or the main true movement of the market.

"It is with these facts well in mind that the student approaches analysis of the averages, premising that broad conclusions are valueless, on the daily fluctuations and deceptive on the secondary movement, but, possible and helpful on the main movement of the market, and of real barometrical value to general business. It may be said as a matter of record that studies in the price movement, with these facts well in view, published in these columns from time to time and especially in the years before the war, were far oftener right than wrong, and were wrong for the most part when they departed from Dow's sound and scientific rule." (Aug. 8, 1919)

"A sympathetic reader asks if the method of estimating the trend of the stock market by analysis of previous movements

as shown in the industrial and railroad price averages is not empirical? Of course it is, but not entirely so, and the method is far removed from quackery. Any conclusion reached from a number of recorded instances is open to that charge. It depends on the scientific accuracy of the method of indication.

"It admits highly human and obvious limitations. But such as it is, it can honestly claim that it has a quality of forecast which no other business record yet devised has even closely approached." (The Stock Market Barometer)

" A number of students demand from...Dow's theory of the triple market movement, a degree of mathematical and even pictorial accuracy which it neither possesses nor needs." (Oct. 18, 1922)

"They can, of course, find plenty of movements, especially secondary ones, which they think the barometer failed to forecast. What of it? An instrument of any such accuracy as they demand would be a human impossibility, and indeed, I do not think that any of us in the present stage of man's moral development could be trusted with such a certainty. One way to bring about a world smash would be for some thoroughly well-intentioned altruist to take the management of the planet out of the hands of its Creator.

"The stock market barometer is not perfect, or to put it more correctly, the adolescent science of reading it is far from having attained perfection.

"The data of the Weather Bureau are of the highest value, but they do not pretend to predict a dry summer or a mild winter. You and I know from personal experience that the weather in New York is likely to be cold in January and hot in July.

"The law that governs the movement of the stock market...would be equally true of the London Stock Exchange, the

*Paris Bourse, or even the Berlin Boerse. But we may go fur-
ther. The principles underlying that law would be true if
those stock exchanges and ours were wiped out of existence.
They would come into operation again, automatically and
inevitably, with the re-establishment of a free market in securities in any great capital. So far as I know, there has not
been a record corresponding to the Dow-Jones averages kept
by any of the London financial publications. But the stock
market there would have the same quality of forecast which
the New York market has if similar data were available.*

*"The theory makes little of cycles or systems, interesting
and even well-grounded inferences or common fads. It uses
them all so far as they are useful, together with every other
scrap of information it is possible to collect. The market movement reflects all the real knowledge available.*

*"...the pragmatic basis for the theory, a working hypothesis
if nothing more, lies in human nature itself. Prosperity will
drive men to excess, and repentance for the consequences of
those excesses will produce a corresponding depression.
Following the dark hour of absolute panic, labor will be
thankful for what it can get and will save slowly out of small-
er wages, while capital will be content with small profits and
quick returns.*

*"When, in the United States Senate, the late Senator
Spooner, reading an editorial of The Wall Street Journal, said,
'Listen to the bloodless verdict of the marketplace,' he saw the
merciless accuracy of that verdict; because it is, and necessarily must be, based upon all the evidence, even when given by
unconscious and unwilling witnesses."* [3]

The Dow Theory is most useful for determining changes in
the major, or "primary," trend in the stock market. The theory is
based on three basic assumptions:

- *The averages discount everything.*
- *Price action determines the trend.*
- *The averages must confirm.*

Robert Rhea explains the first, and most famous, tenet of the Dow Theory succinctly:

"The fluctuations of the daily closing prices of the Dow-Jones rail [Transportation] and Industrial averages afford a composite index of all the hopes, disappointments, and knowledge of everyone who knows anything of financial matters, and for that reason the effects of coming events (excluding acts of God) are always properly anticipated in their movement. The averages quickly appraise such calamities as fires and earthquakes." [4]

This point cannot be emphasized enough. It is commonly believed by most investors that markets are influenced by exogenous events (such as interest rates, significant political and social events, and other such fundamental factors) and that the movements of the market are accounted thereby. The experienced investor, however, knows better. He knows that these outside influences and exogenous factors, far from being *causes* of market trends are instead *manifestations* of the same. This point has been carefully elucidated by Hamilton and Rhea themselves, and more recently by Robert Prechter, editor of *The Elliott Wave Theorist:*

"Market psychology is not responsive. It is not the result of events outside the market. Collective psychology is impulsive, self-generating, self-sustaining and self-reversing...the market is the direct recording of the psychology that later creates the future." [5]

Hamilton elaborates on this principle thusly:

"It is the constant phrase of the Street that a movement is over 'when the news is out.' Stockholders and intelligent speculators operate not on what everybody knows, but on what they alone know or intelligently anticipate. We have often had the spectacle of a general decline in the market, only followed six months afterwards by a contraction in business, or a general advance in the market anticipating by an equal time improving industrial conditions not then obvious.

"...Speculation in stocks itself creates exactly the confidence which stimulates an expansion of general business. This is really only another way of saying that the stock market is a barometer, acting not upon the news of the day, but upon what the combined intelligence of the business world can anticipate."[6]

Stated another way, we may say that 'the news doesn't make the market; the market makes the news.' The stock market (unlike the humans which aggregately compose it) is not reactive in nature. It does not respond to exogenous events such as current news and developments. It anticipates them and responds before the events even happen.

The second most important tenet of the Dow Theory is 'price action determines the trend.' Martin Pring, in his book, *Technical Analysis Explained*, expounds on this by pointing out that "[b]ullish indications are given when successive rallies penetrate peaks while the trough of an intervening decline is above the preceding trough. Conversely, bearish indications come from a series of declining peaks and troughs."[7]

Rhea explains it thusly:

"Successive rallies penetrating preceding high points, with ensuing declines terminating above preceding low points, offer a bullish indication. Conversely, failure of the rallies to penetrate previous high points, with ensuing declines carrying below former low points, is bearish. Inferences so drawn are useful in appraising secondary reactions and are of major importance in forecasting the resumption, continuation, or change of the primary trend. For the purpose of this discussion, a rally or a decline is defined as one or more daily movements resulting in a net reversal of direction exceeding three percent of the price of either average. Such movements have but little authority unless confirmed in direction by both averages, but the confirmation need not occur on the same day."[8]

Rhea goes on to emphasize that a new high or low by one average, unconfirmed by the other, is deceptive.[9] Thus, in the words of Hamilton,

"...On the well-tested rule of reading the averages, a major bull swing continues so long as the rally from a secondary reaction establishes new high points on the same day, or even in the same week, provided only that they confirm each other."[10]

This leads to our third basic tenet: "The averages must confirm." This rule is probably the most important one of the entire Dow Theory, the central tenet on which the efficacy and reliability of the theory hang. Says Rhea:

"The fluctuations of the daily closing prices of the Dow Jones rail [transportation] and industrial averages afford a composite index of all the hopes, disappointments, and knowledge of everyone who knows anything of financial matters, and for that reason the effects of coming events (excluding acts of God) are always properly discounted in their movements. The averages quickly appraise such calamities as fires and earthquakes."[11]

When major news events which command the attention of the entire nation, or even the whole world, fail to rattle the stock market, people invariable shake their heads in utter disbelief that "the news had no effect on the market," never once realizing that the market is not reactive in nature but has instead long since discounted the "news" (a misnomer if ever there was one as the "news" is old hat to the market by the time it is broken to the masses).

Hamilton does an even better job of explaining this:

"The superficial observer is constantly startled to find that the stock market fails to respond to sudden and important developments; while it seems to be guided by impulses too obscure to be traceable. Consciously or unconsciously, the

movements of prices reflect not the past but the future. When coming events cast their shadows before, the shadow falls on the New York Stock Exchange."[12]

And again,

"The market does not trade upon what everybody knows, but upon what those with the best information can foresee. There is an explanation for every stock market movement somewhere in the future, and the much talked of manipulation is a trifling factor."[13]

This principle, at once so simple and profound in its import, is missed by the vast majority of investors and therefore leads to much unnecessary losses from investment decisions based on some news event or "hot tip." Indeed, investors ignore this principle to their peril.

There are many other aspects of the Dow Theory that, while important complements of the theory and useful to know, are not crucial to a basic understanding of it. Everything that is necessary for an investor or an analyst to know, we believe, can be summarized in the foregoing three basic tenets of the Dow Theory. However, for the serious student of the market, a deeper study of the Dow Theory is recommended.

We agree with Rhea that "[a] complete understanding of the necessity of waiting for confirmation by both averages is absolutely necessary if the Dow theory is to be used advantageously." [14] In expounding upon this point we quote extensively from Hamilton's views on the subject:

"Dow always ignored a movement of one average which was not confirmed by the other, and experience since his death has shown the wisdom of that method of checking the reading of the averages. His theory was that a downward movement of secondary, and perhaps ultimately primary importance was established when the new lows for both averages were under the low points of the preceding reaction." [15]

"It is no light matter to manipulate both averages, and the indications of one without the other are generally disregarded." [16]

"It seems a clear inference, in a movement where the averages do not confirm each other, than uncertainty still continues as concerns the business outlook..." [17]

"There is one fairly safe rule about reading the averages, even if it is a negative one. This is that half an indication is not necessarily better than no indication at all. The two averages must confirm each other..." [18]

"A new low or a new high made by the one but not confirmed by the other is almost invariably deceptive. One group of securities acts upon the other; and if the market for railroad stocks is sold out it cannot lift the whole list with it if there is a superabundant supply of the industrials." [19]

Notes

[1] Written in 1932

[2] Rhea, Robert, The Dow Theory, Fraser Publishing Co., 1993, pg. 1

[3] Ibid, pg. 8

[4] Ibid., pg. 12

[5] Prechter, Robert, Prechter's Perspective, New Classics Library, 1996

[6] Rhea, pg. 22

[7] Ibid., pg. 36

[8] Ibid., pg. 75

[9] Ibid., pg. 75

[10] Ibid., pg. 189

[11] Ibid., pg. 152

[12] Ibid., pg. 70

[13] Ibid., pg. 238
[14] Ibid., pg. 209
[15] Ibid., pg. 239
[16] Ibid., pg. 169
[17] Ibid., pg. 169
[18] Ibid., pg. 170
[19] Ibid., pg. 170

Chapter 3

Pattern Recognition

"...pattern recognition [is] the chief strength of the human mind over a computer. An ant on an eagle's head will still not see patterns in the valley below because neither his eyes nor his mind are made for it."

—P.Q. Wall

Now that we have established a firm foundation with the Dow Theory, we may proceed to what we consider to be the single most important element of chart analysis: pattern recognition. This forms the basis of all technical analysis and is absolutely essential to being able to identify and forecast market trends.

First, let's define what we mean by our choice of this term. By pattern recognition, we mean the ability to recognize geometric shapes formed by the price of a security on its chart. This "price action," as it has been called, forms the basis for technical analysis. It is a known fact that speculative activity in the marketplace (the buying and selling of securities by many participants) visibly manifests itself on the charts of actively traded securities. The very action of trading shares in a particular stock or commodity registers on paper as a geometric pattern of some sort, based on historical precedent. If then these historical patterns can be recognized it affords the analyst with an opportunity to profit from them.

It is important to note that only securities that are widely traded produce the most discernible, and hence, the most reliable, chart patterns. The very act of a given security trading among thousands or even millions of market participants creates the condition known as "liquidity," defined as the ease of being able to buy or sell, or enter or exit a security. The more liquidity a security has, the more reliable its chart pattern will be. So the first thing a good technical analyst looks for in a security is the volume of trade in that particular share (we will cover this in greater detail in a later chapter).

When a security with a reasonable amount of liquidity is traded in the marketplace, observable patterns will form in its chart. These patterns normally have historical significance and, if recognized, can be used to forecast the future trend (and sometimes even the actual future price) of the security. Our job as technical analysts, then, is one of discovery and interpretation of chart patterns.

Chart patterns take one of two varieties: continuation formations or reversal formations. For the making of large profits—not to mention preserving working capital—identifying reversal patterns is the most important trait a technical analyst can learn.

This is an acquired skill that is learned only through assiduous study of chart patterns and general experience, but once acquired, the advantages are immense.

The reality of market trends, however, is that at any given time in any given security, the trend is usually in the form of a continuation pattern. So it becomes equally important to be able to identify continuation patterns, which also have forecasting value.

At this point it becomes necessary to introduce another set of technical terms which correspond to the two basic types of patterns. These terms are used to describe the overall trend of the market, that is, an impulsive or corrective trend.

By impulsive, we refer to the direction the market takes when it is traveling decisively in a certain direction—either up or down. In other words, the overall thrust of the market. In Dow Theory parlance, a primary bear market is a downward impulsive move while a primary bull market is upward impulsive. An impulsive move corresponds to a continuation formation.

A corrective market is a market trend that involves either a temporary reversal of the prevailing trend and a partial retracement (usually anywhere from one-third to two-thirds). A corrective pattern (i.e., a "correction") can also take the form of a net sideways movement, also known as a consolidation (a "line" in Dow Theory). A corrective movement corresponds to a reversal formation.

Reversal Patterns

We will start with those chart patterns that reverse market trends. Our first pattern is perhaps the most famous of all chart patterns if only because of its unusual name—the head and shoulders pattern (H&S).

The H&S pattern, besides being well-known, is also one of the most reliable of all chart patterns. Its name is derived from its appearance on the chart. It consists of three peaks and two troughs. The extreme right and left peaks (the "shoulders") are as a rule lower than the center peak (the "head"). Each H&S pattern also has a "neckline" which is a hypothetical line drawn directly beneath the pattern and touching the base of all three peaks. Although the pattern typically takes the common form of one head, one left shoulder, and one right shoulder, it can

Head & Shoulders Top Reversal

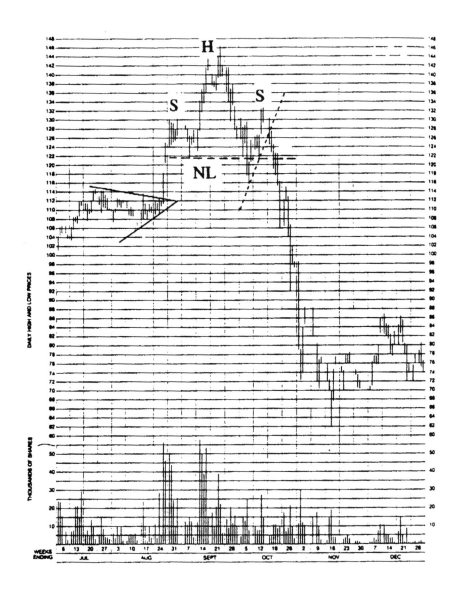

Head & Shoulders Bottom Reversal

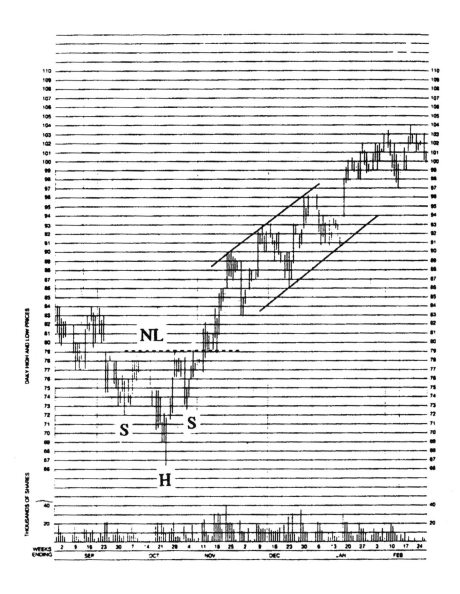

also be of the complex variety wherein multiple heads and shoulders develop.

During bull markets an H&S pattern that develops on the charts forecasts a reversal of trend in the opposite direction (i.e., downward). The amplitude of the trend can also be forecast by measuring the distance between the neckline and the top of the "head." This very often provides the minimum distance prices will travel before the trend is complete. Thus, if an H&S top pattern develops in a particular stock chart with the absolute top of the head at, say, $50 a share and the neckline at $40 a share, the stock can be expected to travel to $30 a share before consolidating or reversing higher (though prices often travel even further below the minimum measuring implications).

In the bottom position, the H&S pattern is identical to the H&S top formation, only turned upside down. Its measuring implications are the same (from the top of the head to the neckline). The H&S bottom formation only occurs after a sustained downtrend and signals a bottom and reversal higher, once the pattern is complete.

While the H&S pattern itself is very reliable, it must still be confirmed by trading volume. In the top position the H&S typically has high volume while the left shoulder is forming, diminishing volume during formation of the head and even less volume while the right shoulder is forming. A "breakout" is confirmed when prices fall through the neckline by at least 3% accompanied by a significant increase in volume (the three percent rule was developed by Edwards & Magee and has proved reliable over the years).

In the bottom position the H&S is confirmed by high volume on the left shoulder, lower volume on the head, and higher volume on the right shoulder (often equal to the volume during formation of the left shoulder). A breakout is confirmed, again, by a 3% penetration of the neckline made on high volume.

While the H&S pattern is classified as a reversal phenomenon, it can sometimes signify a continuation of the prevailing trend. This is usually very easily distinguished by noting the position of the H&S. As a continuation pattern the H&S will take the opposite position of what it should during a particular move. Thus, in an uptrending market an H&S will be in the bottom formation (with the peaks of the head and shoulders pointing downward instead of upward). But instead of signifying a bottom it merely represents a temporary consolidation of the prevailing trend before it continues its previous course. (For a pictorial example of the H&S continuation pattern, see illustration). In a downward trending market the H&S continuation pattern takes the form of an H&S top pattern with all three peaks of the head and two shoulders pointing upward. It is clearly distinguished from an H&S reversal pattern because the upward pointing H&S pattern occurs following a sustained downtrend rather than an uptrend. However, its minimum measuring implications remain identical to that of the true H&S top.

H&S patterns may occur in weekly, daily, and even intraday charts but rarely in monthly charts. The appearance of this pattern in any chart whatsoever should be duly noted by the technical analyst and followed closely throughout its development, making sure to check trading volume to see if it corresponds with the pattern's development.

The most important rule of thumb to help the analyst determine whether an H&S pattern is of the reversal or continuation variety is to remember that a reversal pattern must have something to reverse.

Rounding Formations

Turning our attention to another reversal phenomenon, we come now to the series of patterns known as rounding reversals. These patterns may either reverse market trends at tops or at bottoms; hence, their designations as rounding tops and rounding bottoms.

Rounding tops, as their name suggests, resemble domes or semi-circles in appearance. They are also known as rounding turns or common turns. Rounding bottoms form a bowl-shaped pattern known variously as saucer bottoms or tea cups.

Of all reversal patterns, rounding formations are the easiest to identify (although their occurrence is somewhat less frequent than that of the head and shoulders pattern). In reality, however, the rounding formations are usually nothing more than complex head and shoulders patterns drawn out over a longer period than normal for the standard H&S.

Both the rounding top and the rounding bottom pattern are accompanied by greatly diminished volume throughout the formation of the bowl or saucer, with a significant increase in volume as prices advance beyond the sides of the bowl. Much like the H&S, a hypothetical "neckline" may be drawn at the top of the bowl connecting both sides of the bowl. When prices advance beyond this line by at least 3% on increase volume, a breakout is confirmed. As with the H&S, the bowl formation contains its own measuring implications that may be used to forecast the amplitude of the market's subsequent breakout. This is derived by measuring the distance between the top and bottom of the bowl and adding that difference (as measured in share price) to the top of the bowl. This will normally project the absolute minimum that prices will carry before either reversing or consolidating (and it usually carries farther than that).

It should also be noted that prices often reverse slightly lower once they have emerged from completely forming the bowl. To the untrained eye this appears to be a complete failure of the pattern but in reality it is merely a normal pullback as prices gather steam for a final breakout through the top of the bowl. This gives the appearance on the chart of a teacup, with the pullback taking on the appearance of the "handle" after the "cup" has been formed (see example).

Rounding Top

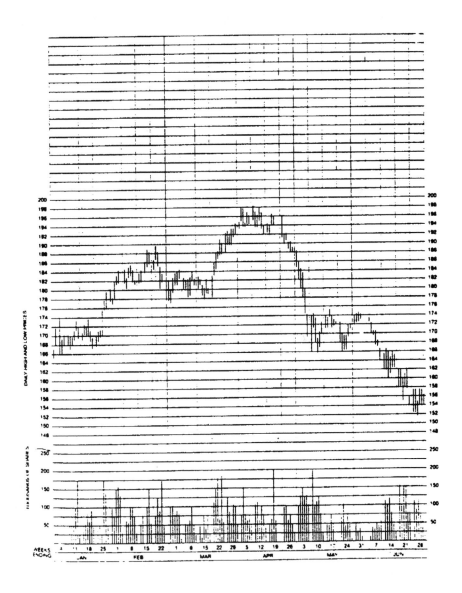

Rounding Bottom

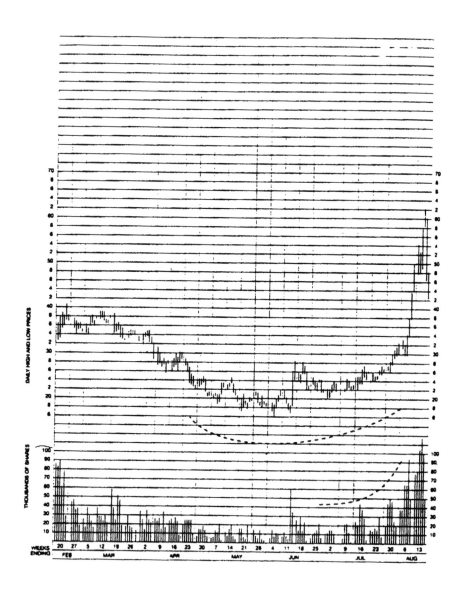

Triangles

Next we will examine a group of related chart patterns that may occur as either reversal or continuation formations: the triangle family.

Unlike the previous patterns we've studied, triangles, while easy to spot, do not always let the analyst know beforehand where prices will carry upon completion of the triangulation of prices in the chart. Their utility to the analyst consists in providing an advanced warning that a decisive breakout is coming once the consolidation of prices on the chart is complete. Like the other patterns, triangles also provide the analyst with a formula for measuring the amplitude of future price movement once the triangle has been "broken."

The first triangle pattern we will look at is the symmetrical triangle, otherwise known as the contracting triangle. A symmetrical triangle is composed of a series of fluctuations having a lower peak and a higher low than the preceding one. It is graphically illustrated on a chart as a triangle having an apex or tip pointing to the right with the upper and lower boundaries at equilateral gradients to one another (see example).

While it can be a reversal pattern it more regularly occurs as a continuation pattern. Its minimum price carrying implications can be found by measuring the distance between the extreme high and low points of upper and lower boundary lines, respectively. That difference (measured in terms of price) should then be added onto the apex and will normally produce the minimum amplitude prices will carry upon breaking out of the triangle.

One additional feature of symmetrical triangles (indeed, of any of the various types of triangles we will cover that should be remembered) is that prices within a triangle will, on balance, alternately bounce from the lower to upper boundaries of the triangle a total of five times before breaking out of it. This is what R.W. Schabacker called the "Rule of Five." This remarkable rule also has application in many other technical patterns as we will see later.

Volume throughout the formation of the symmetrical triangle should be diminishing as prices reach the apex. A breakout from the boundaries of the triangle, to either the upside or downside, should be accompanied by a dramatic increase in volume. As a general rule, prices usually follow through in the direction they took in breaking out of the triangle.

Right-Angle Triangles

Our next class of triangles differ from the symmetrical triangle in that their directional implications—be it bullish or bearish—can normally be inferred from the position the hypotenuse takes.

In the ascending position (known as ascending triangles), the hypotenuse should be upward sloping with a perfectly level upper boundary line. Because the hypotenuse is upward sloping this implies prices will climb higher in the direction of the slope once the consolidation within the boundaries of the triangle is complete. As with the symmetrical triangle, volume should be considerably lower when forming and noticeably higher at the time of the breakout. Although ascending triangles may be regarded as a reversal pattern (typically occurring in downward trending markets and signaling a reversal higher) they may also appear as continuation patterns in bull markets.

The Rule of Five is also applicable with ascending triangles as it is with those of the symmetrical variety. The minimum measuring implications are also the same, that is, measuring the distance between the widest ends of the triangle and adding that difference in price to the upper boundary line.

The other manifestation of the right-angle triangle, the descending triangle, is of bearish import. It is distinguished from the ascending triangle by its downward sloping hypotenuse and horizontal lower boundary. It typically occurs

Symmetrical Triangle

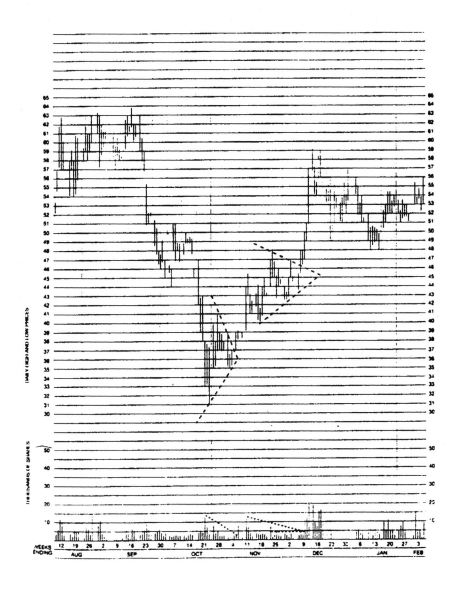

at the top of a long rise in prices and portends a decline in share price once the pattern is complete.

Like the ascending and symmetrical varieties, descending triangles should have greatly diminished volume during their formation and should be punctuated by a hefty pickup in volume once prices break out of the pattern.

The Rule of Five is applicable to this pattern (though it is important to point out that this rule does not have to be perfectly fulfilled-prices may sometimes touch the upper and lower boundaries of the triangle more than or less than five times-but as a rule it generally is fulfilled). The measuring implications for this pattern are also the same as for the other triangles.

Because the descending triangle may sometimes occur as a continuation pattern it is important to remember that the direction prices take on breaking out of the pattern is the direction the trader should follow.

Before proceeding further we also want to point out another important rule of chart pattern analysis. In any given chart pattern, regardless of the geometric shape prices take on the chart, the upper boundary line of the pattern that acts to contain prices within the developing chart pattern is known as the "resistance level." Resistance levels also correspond to the supply aspect in the supply/demand relationship that lies at the crux of any security.

The lower boundary line of any chart pattern is known in technical parlance as the "support" level and corresponds to demand in the supply/demand relationship. Thus, chart patterns serve as pictorial representations of supply and demand, or more particularly, the balance of supply and demand.

In a triangle pattern the upper boundary, or resistance, represents supply while the lower boundary, or support, represents demand. So when we see, for example, a symmetrical triangle

Ascending Triangle

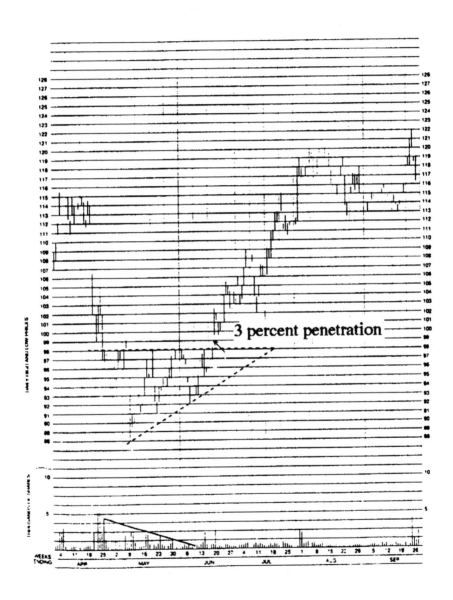

Descending Triangle

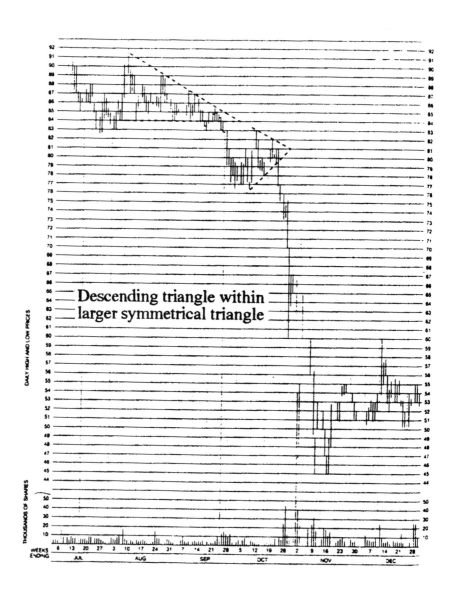

Descending triangle within larger symmetrical triangle

forming on the charts what we are really seeing is the relative balance between supply and demand. If the symmetrical triangle is contracting throughout its formation, that means both supply and demand are contracting at equal degrees in the marketplace and a battle between buyers and sellers is shaping up. When prices reach the extreme point, or apex, of the wedge the battle between buyers and sellers has reached a crescendo and supply and demand have reached a point of equilibrium. Prices must respond by either shooting rapidly upward or downward, depending on market conditions.

In the case of the ascending triangle the upward sloping hypotenuse translates into a rising demand since the lower boundary line, or support, is rising while the horizontal upper boundary, or resistance (representing supply) remains constant. A rising demand for a security with a steady supply generally means higher prices, as the pattern infers.

Conversely, with a descending triangle the supply line (resistance) is sloping downward while demand (support) remains steady. Falling supply with a steady demand, of course, translates in most cases into falling prices as indeed this pattern usually portends.

Other Classifications

We come now to an entirely different series of chart patterns which, while similar in appearance to the triangles we have just examined, are much different in many respects. Because of these differences classical technical analysis classifies them under a separate rubric, that of pennants and wedges.

The pennant is similar in appearance to the symmetrical triangle in that it is bounded by converging boundary lines which meet at the apex to form a distinctly triangular-shaped pattern. It slants downward when it appears in an uptrend, and upwards in a downtrend.[1] In many respects it is similar to a "flag" pattern, a formation we will discuss later. Edwards & Magee describe it further:

"It forms, as a rule, after a rapid advance (or decline), and trading volume shrinks notably during its construction. In fact, [trading volume] tends to diminish...rapidly in a pennant...and may drop almost to nothing before the pennant is completed and prices break away from it in a new and rapid move." [2]

It is similar to a wedge (a pattern we will take up next) except that it is shorter and much more compact. Its forecasting implications are much different from that of a triangle. The simple rule of measurement for a pennant is that prices will generally return to the level they were at when the pennant first began forming. In other words, prices can be expected to retrace all of their preceding losses while the wedge formed. This is only the minimum measuring expectation; prices usually carry even further beyond this point.

One final characteristic of the pennant that should be noted is that when prices move out of the pennant, they ordinarily do so not in a sudden straight-line breakaway but rather in an accelerating curve with volume increasing gradually instead of abruptly at the break. [3] The whole pattern, as Edwards & Magee point out, resembles a curved horn which runs to a long, slender point. [4]

A close cousin to the pennant is the falling wedge, which is identical in all points to the pennant with one exception: it is much longer and narrower and takes a greater length of time to form on the charts. Much like the pennant, the wedge may appear in either the rising or falling form.

In its rising form, known simply as "rising wedge" or "ascending wedge," it forecasts a move in the opposite direction from which the wedge is pointed. In the case of the rising wedge prices will fall rapidly upon completion, while prices will gradually move higher once a falling wedge is complete. This represents a difference from the rising wedge-prices may take several days to weeks to head higher once they break out of the apex

Pennant

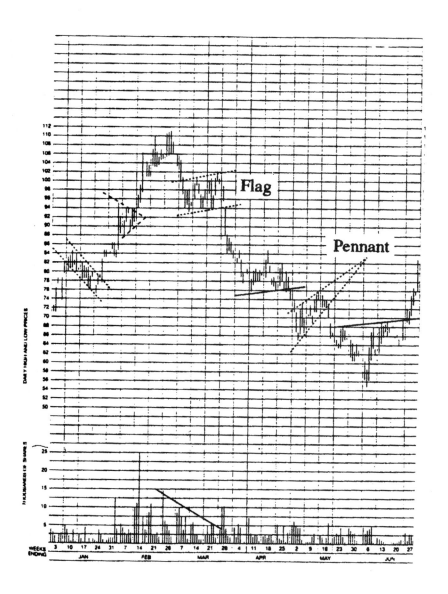

Rising Wedge

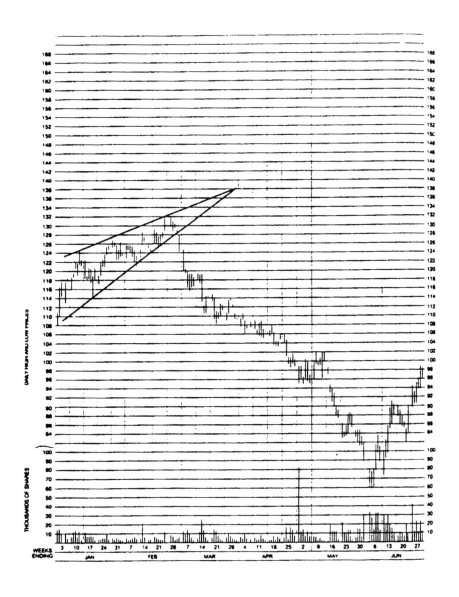

Falling Wedge

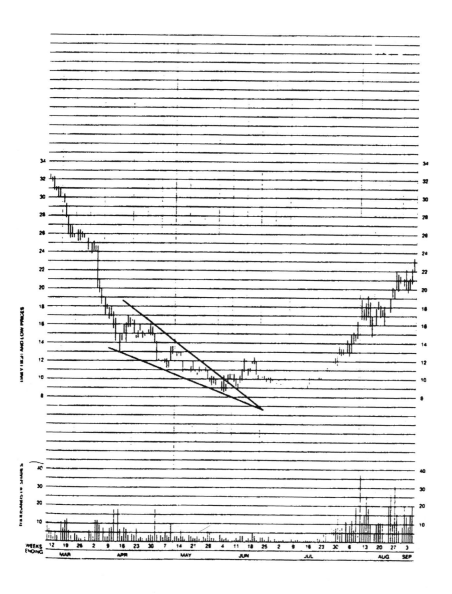

of the falling wedge and proceed in a meandering sideways pattern before beginning to move decisively upward. With the rising wedge, prices usually fall very rapidly once the apex has been reached.

The Rule of Five applies here as well but prices often alternately touch the upper and lower boundary lines more than five times in a wedge pattern.

As with the other triangle patterns, volume should be rapidly diminishing throughout the formation of this pattern until a breakout occurs on high volume. Measuring implications for either type of wedge is the same as that of the pennant formation.

Inverted Triangles

One further pattern in the triangle family is the inverted triangle, known also as a broadening formation. There are three distinctive types of this pattern with one of them, the "broadening top," occurring only at market tops and forecasting a reversal lower. The other two inverted triangle patterns may occur as either reversal or continuation patterns.

The broadening top, which equates to a reversed symmetrical triangle (and is sometimes called by this name) forecasts a reversal in the market. The apex points to the extreme left rather than the extreme right as with other triangles and the upper and lower boundaries widen to form a "mouth" from which prices fall upon reaching the end of the pattern. The Rule of Five applies in this pattern.

The broadening top, which occurs far less frequently than the other triangle patterns, is particularly ominous because its overhead resistance line is moving higher, indicating increasing supply. Meanwhile, its support level is falling indicating falling demand. This acts as a "double whammy" and, in most cases, ensures a rather nasty decline in share price.

Unlike the other triangle phenomena, trading volume should be increasing rather than decreasing throughout the formation of this pattern.

Edwards & Magee describe it this way:

"The Orthodox Broadening Top has three peaks at successively higher levels and, between them, two bottoms with the second bottom lower than the first. The assumption has been that it is completed and in effect is an important reversal indication just as soon as the reaction from its third peak carries below the level of its second bottom." [5]

The right-angle broadening formation, another class of inverted triangle, consists of either a horizontal supply line and downward sloping hypotenuse or a horizontal demand line with an upward sloping hypotenuse. The latter type frequently occurs as a bearish reversal pattern at the end of a long rise in prices. The former manifestation may occur as either a bearish reversal pattern or a bullish continuation pattern with the latter of these appearing most often. Volume characteristics are the same for the reverse symmetrical triangle. A breakout (to either the upside or downside of this pattern) should penetrate the pattern by roughly 3% and should be accompanied by a significant increase in trading volume.

Finally, we include in our discussion of broadening formations a very unusual and rare pattern of this family, known as a diamond reversal formation. As its name implies, it occurs only as a reversal pattern at either tops or bottoms and indicates a change of trend is at hand. It may be described as either a complex head and shoulders pattern with a V-shaped neckline, or as a broadening formation consisting of two successive symmetrical triangles-the first in the inverted form and the second in the orthodox form. Coming together as they do they form a diamond-shaped pattern when lines are drawn connecting the relevant points on the chart.

Although it can occur at bottoms it occurs much more frequently at tops. Its volume characteristics are identical to that of the head and shoulders pattern-high volume on the left-hand side of the pattern, lower volume in the center, and even lower volume on the right-hand side just before the breakout occurs (which, as with the other patterns, should occur on high volume with prices moving away from the pattern by at least 3% before being considered legitimate).

The minimum measuring implications for the diamond reversal pattern are similar to that for the orthodox H&S pattern; that is, prices should move at least as far from the breakout point as the greatest width in points of the pattern from its top (head) to bottom ("V" in neckline). [6]

Broadening Top

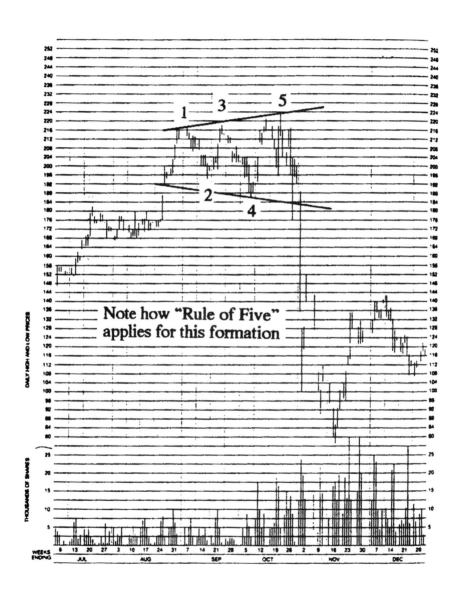

Note how "Rule of Five" applies for this formation

Rectangles

Our next group of patterns fall under the broad classification of rectangles due to their rectangular appearance. They sometimes represent reversals of trend, but generally are classified as continuation patterns.

The first pattern we will take up is actually called a rectangle. It consists of a series of sideways price fluctuations-a "trading area," as it is sometimes called-which can be bounded both top and bottom by horizontal lines. [7]

As a general rule, trading volume as the rectangle is forming should be relatively light, though not necessarily as light as volume during the formation of triangle patterns. As with triangles, a breakout is confirmed when prices exceed either the upper or lower boundary line by at least 3% on high volume.

The Rule of Five is applicable with rectangles (though prices may alternate from top to bottom more than five times before breaking out and are by no means bound by this rule).

A good measuring formula that we have discovered for the rectangle is to measure the distance between upper and lower boundary lines in terms of price. Then multiply that number by five (from the Rule of Five) and then add the product onto either the top or bottom boundary line (depending upon from which level prices break out). That number usually provides a reliable approximation as to minimum price target.

In Dow Theory, rectangles correspond to "line" and are deemed by Dow Theorists to be of great significance, so much so that Rhea conferred upon them axiom, rather than theorem, status. He designated lines as follows:

"A 'line' is a price movement extending two or three weeks or longer, during which price variations of both averages move within a range of approximately five percent. Such a movement indicates either accumulation or distribution.

Rectangle

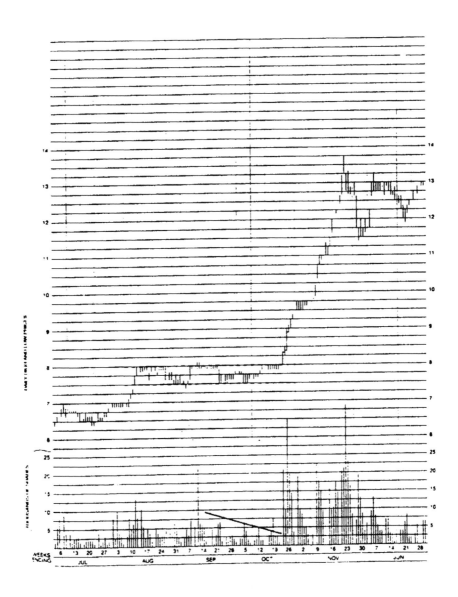

Simultaneous advances above the limits of the 'line' indicate accumulation and predict higher prices; conversely, simultaneous declines below the 'line' imply distribution and lower prices are sure to follow. Conclusions drawn from the movement of one average, not confirmed by the other, generally prove to be incorrect." [8]

As with the other patterns in the rectangle group, the rectangle, or "line" itself may either be a reversal or a continuation pattern.

Our next pattern, a "flag," gets its name obviously from its resemblance to a flag on the chart. If it appears in an uptrend the flag, which consists of a short, narrow rectangle, typically appears at a slight angular slope in the opposite direction of the trend (similar to the wedge formations). It usually occurs as a period of brief consolidation—typically lasting no longer than three to four days, and normally forecasts a rather lengthy runup in price. To the trained observer, flags are magnificent warnings signs of great profit potential shortly ahead.

Although the flag in an uptrend generally points downward, it may also appear with a slight upward slope (though this is uncommon). In fact, it may also develop as a series of successive bowl-shaped formations with a short "flag pole" between them, known as "scallops." This pattern is really a form of flag. In a downward trend, of course, this picture is reversed and the flag points slightly upward in counter-trend fashion. Both patterns harbinger a continuation of the prevailing trend once the consolidation is over.

Volume during the formation of a flag should be considerably lower than during the time preceding its formation and normally diminishes during each day of its formation until a breakout is signaled by high volume and a 3 percent penetration of the flag.

A pattern very similar to the flag, known as a "half mast," shares all the characteristics of a flag but with two subtle dis-

Flag

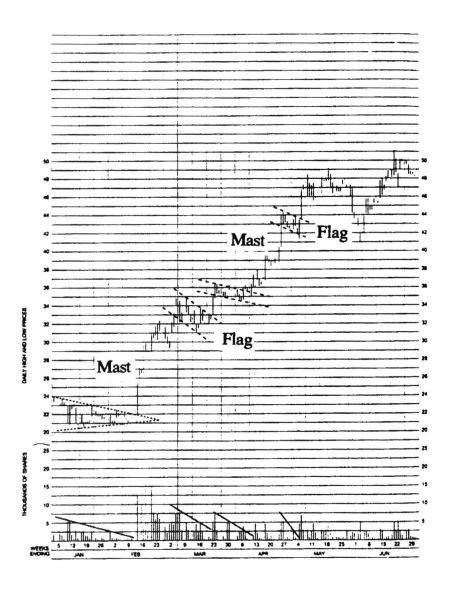

tinctions: the "flag" consolidation is perfectly straight instead of slanted (resembling a very short, compact square or rectangle on the charts) and is preceded in most cases by an almost perfectly vertical upmove in price. The vertical price line on the chart thus gives the appearance of a flag pole, or mast, and a small flag forms on low volume, followed by yet another "mast" more or less equal in length to the previous one.

The minimum measuring implications for both the flag and half mast patterns is simple. The "mast," or price trend preceding the formation of the flag, should be measured in terms of price. That number is then added on to the level of prices at the point of breakout from the flag.

These patterns typically develop during the "runaway" portion of either a bull market or a bear market and can be used by the analyst for making rapid profits with relatively low risk due to the reliability of the patterns.

It is important to recognize that variations to each of the patterns discussed in this chapter exist and that there is no guarantee of a textbook perfect pattern in real-time charts. However, possessing a thorough knowledge of the basic chart patterns along with much practice will enable any trader to apply these principles to almost any chart pattern and profit thereby.

Half Mast

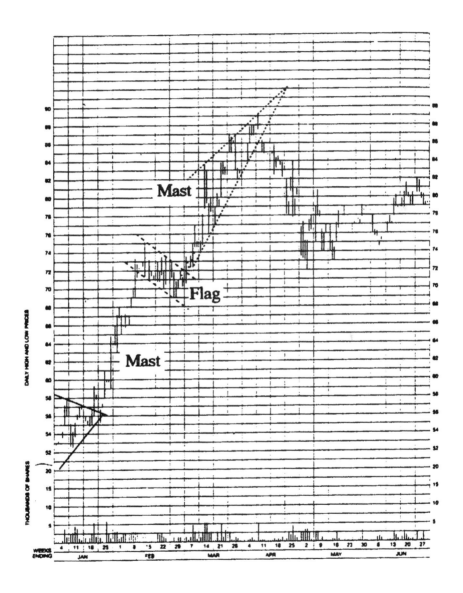

Notes

[1] Edwards & Magee, *Technical Analysis of Stock Trends,*
Amacom, 1948, 1997, pg. 209

[2] Ibid., pg. 209

[3] Ibid., pg. 210

[4] Ibid., pg. 211-212

[5] Ibid., pg. 173-175

[6] Ibid., pg. 185

[7] Ibid., pg. 141

[8] Rhea, Robert, *The Dow Theory,* Fraser Publishing Co., 1993,
pg. 79

[9] Ibid., pg. 189

[10] Ibid., pg. 152

[11] Ibid., pg. 70

Chapter 4

Volume

After examining the various chart patterns in the previous chapter, you have noticed by now that emphasis has been heavily placed on trading volume in determining the validity of any given chart pattern. In fact, no chart pattern should be given full credibility until it can be shown that the trading volume accompanying those chart formations is commensurate with their proper volume patterns.

What do we mean by trading volume? Simply put, volume represents the number of contracts traded over a period of time in any given security. As a technical indicator, volume provides important clues as to both investor sentiment as well as what is happening with a given chart pattern.

Basically, volume should increase—or at least stabilize—in the direction of the price trend. If the prevailing trend is up, volume should be heavier on the up days and lighter on the down days. If the trend was down, volume should be heavier on the down days, with lighter volume on the up days. This is because in an uptrend there should be more buyers than sellers, and in a downtrend there should be more sellers than buyers. If volume should start to diminish, it would be a warning that the trend could be losing steam and that a consolidation or perhaps a reversal could be ahead. If the trend is up, and we now see more volume on dips than on rallies, it should be an alert that buying pressure is waning and sellers are becoming more aggressive. The reverse would be true in a downtrend. If volume starts to shrink on the sell-offs and picks up on the rallies, once again, it could be a sign that the trend is in trouble, and buyers are starting to assert themselves. When volume moves in the opposite direction of the price, this is called divergence.

One of the reasons why volume has a tendency to diminish during periods of indecision is for just that reason. During periods of lateral movement on the charts, traders will often avoid a market, preferring to stay on the sidelines and commit their funds only when a clear-cut breakout develops. However, while it is typical for volume to diminish during these times, volume can give clues as to possible future direction by measuring the level of conviction of the buyers and the sellers. Seeing if there is heavier volume on the up days or on the down days, the buyers are probably the more aggressive and the market should break out to the upside. The reverse is true if the volume is heavier on the down days, with the market likely to break out to the downside.

Addressing the relation of volume to price movements, Rhea writes:

"A market which has been overbought becomes dull on rallies and develops activity on declines; conversely, when a market is oversold, the tendency is to become dull on declines and active on rallies. Bull markets terminate in a period of excessive activity and begin with comparatively light transactions." [1]

He writes further:

"Examination of charts of the daily movements of the averages and volume of trading over a long period of years

demonstrates that the tendency is for volume to increase whenever new highs or new lows have been made in primary bull or bear markets, with such a increase frequently progressing until something like a climax indicates a temporary reversal of the movement." [2]

Rhea concludes:

"In emphasizing the importance of volume, the writer does not, of course, intend to convey the idea that volume of trading is as important as the movements of the industrial and [transportation] averages. The latter are always to be considered as of primary importance. Volume is of secondary significance, but it should never be overlooked when a study is being made of the price movement." [3]

Martin Pring, in *Technical Analysis Explained*, expounds upon the traditional concept of volume as a price trend corroborator by demonstrating it can also serve as a price indicator. Quoting William Gordon, author of *The Stock Market Indicators*, he writes:

"In 84 percent of the bull markets the volume high did not occur at the price peak but some months before." [4]

Pring notes that volume "has an almost consistent tendency to peak out ahead of price during both bull and bear phases." [5] He concludes that volume "gives strong indications of a trend reversal when it moves in the opposite direction to the prevailing trend." [6]

Notes

[1] Rhea, Robert, *The Dow Theory*, Fraser Publishing Co., 1993, pg. 86
[2] Ibid., pg. 89
[3] Ibid., pg. 92
[4] Pring, Martin, Technical Analysis Explained, McGraw-Hill, 1990, 1994, pg. 273
[5] Ibid., pg. 288
[6] Ibid, pg. 288

Chapter 5
Breadth

Market breadth, as measured by the ratio of advancing issues versus declining issues, measures the degree to which issues that constitute the market are participating in a market move. As such, breadth serves as a reliable gauge of the underlying strength of a market trend.

In a bull market, for instance, confirmation of the strength of the trend should be reflected in the advance/decline line; that is, the great majority of issues should be advancing with comparatively fewer declining issues. The reverse holds true in bear markets.

Along with volume, breadth serves as one of the most basic and effective market indicators and, as a corollary to the Dow Theory concept of the confirmation of the averages, should be used as a confirmation of the strength behind a market trend (be it bullish or bearish). Simply put, the great majority of market issues should be strongly participating in the established trend, whatever that trend may be. Any divergence between breadth and market trend should immediately be viewed with suspicion and will often serve as an indicator that the trend is about to change. Thus, if the market is in an uptrend and breadth begins to deteriorate (i.e., the number of advancing issues begins to lag or even becomes outnumbered by the number of declining issues) that is usually a sign that a trend reversal is imminent.

The most widely used indicator of market breadth is an advance/decline (A/D) line. It is constructed by taking a cumulative total of the difference (plurality) between the number of New York Stock Exchange (NYSE) issues that are advancing over those that are declining in a particular period (usually a day or a week). [1] Similar indexes may be constructed for the American Exchange (AMEX) or from NASDAQ issues.

Martin Pring, in *Technical Analysis Explained,* explains that one of the most useful measurements of breadth is a cumulative running total of the formula square root of A/U - D/U, where A = the number of stocks advancing, D = the number declining, and U = the number unchanged. [2] Since it is not mathematically possible to calculate a square root of a negative answer (i.e., when the number of declining stocks is greater than the number of those advancing, the calculation cannot be done), the D and A are reversed in such cases, so that the formula becomes the square root of D/U - A/U. The resulting answer is then subtracted from the cumulative total, as opposed to the answer in the earlier formula, which is added. [3]

"Inclusion of the number of unchanged issues is useful, because at certain points a more reliable advance warning of an imminent trend reversal in the A/D line can be given," writes Pring. "This is because the more dynamic the move in either direction, the greater the tendency for the number of unchanged stocks to diminish. Consequently, by giving some weight to the number of unchanged stocks in the formula, it is possible to assess a slowdown in momentum of the A/D line at an earlier date, since an expanding number of unchanged issues will have the tendency to restrain extreme movements." [4]

Continues Pring:

"The A/D line normally rises and falls in sympathy with the major market averages, but it usually peaks well ahead of the top in the major averages." [5]

While there exists a wide array of breadth indicators that may be utilized by the trader and merit closer examination, including breadth oscillators, the ARMS index, and the McClellan Oscillator, to name a few, we focus only on the simple A/D line for reasons of simplicity and efficacy. A trader who holds to the K.I.S.S. maxim (Keep It Simple Stupid) is more likely to find success in his endeavors than the one who yields to the temptation to use every new-fangled, computer-generated breadth indicator that comes along. In our experience, the tried-and-true A/D line of the NYSE is the most convenient and reliable measure of breadth for gauging the strength of the broad market and for forecasting turning points. All but the most sophisticated traders will want to stick to it.

Finally, we should note Pring's conclusion concerning the use of breadth indicators in the technical analysis of the market:

"Breadth divergences are a fine concept, but should be confirmed by a trend reversal in the market averages themselves." [6]

Notes

[1] Pring, Martin, *Technical Analysis Explained*, McGraw-Hill, 1990, 1994, pg. 290
[2] Ibid., pg. 290
[3] Ibid., pg. 291
[4] Ibid., pg. 291
[5] Ibid., pg. 291
[6] Ibid., pg. 314

Chapter 6

Reliability of the Chart Patterns

Now that we have laid a firm foundation in being able to identify and interpret chart patterns, the question that immediately is raised is, "Do the chart patterns have validity at all times or can they not be subject to manipulations like other areas of human concern?" After all, if chart patterns can themselves be manipulated by powerful insiders, of what use is it to understand chart pattern analysis when the charts by manipulation prove misleading? In this chapter we will examine these and other such concerns and offer useful hints for recognizing and avoiding manipulation when it occurs (which is fortunately rare), as well as dispel certain myths surrounding the subject.

Edwards & Magee address this dual concern of chart pattern reliability and the possibility for manipulation with remarkable insight. We quote from them at length:

"The charts we make today seem to follow the old patterns; the presumption is very strong that markets have followed these patterns long before there were any technicians to chart them. The differences mentioned [here], due to changed margin requirements, restraining of manipulative practices, etc.,

seem to have changed these habits, if at all, only in degree and not in their fundamental nature.

"The market is big, too big for any person, corporation or combine to control as a speculative unit. Its operation is extremely free and extremely democratic in the sense that it represents the integration of the hopes and fears of many kinds of buyers and sellers. Not all are short-term traders...

"And not all short-term traders are technicians by any manner of means. There are those who trade on fundamentals for the short term; those who rely on tips, hunches, on reading the stars, on personal knowledge of the company. They are all part of the competitive market, they are all using methods different from yours-and sometimes they will be right and you will be wrong.

"The technician using the various tools of technical analysis— Dow Theory, scale order systems, and monthly, weekly, and daily charts—is in the minority. The cold attempt to analyze a situation on the basis of the market record alone does not appeal to many people. Technical analysis leaves out the warmth and human interest of the boardroom, the fascinating rumors of fat extra dividends to come, the whispered information on new patents, and the thrilling story of the quarterly earnings reports.

"It is the influence of all these rumors, facts and statistics that causes men to buy and sell their stocks. It is their actions that build the familiar chart patterns. You are not interested in why they are doing what they are doing. So far as your trading is concerned you are interested only in the results of their actions.

"The habits and evaluative methods of people are deeply ingrained. The same kinds of events produce the same kinds of emotional responses, and hence, the same kinds of market action. These characteristic approaches are extremely durable. It is not quite true that 'you can't change human

nature,' but it is true that it is very difficult to change the per-
ceptive habits of a lifetime. And since the 'orthodox' investors
greatly outnumber the technicians, we may confidently
assume that technical trading will have little or no effect on
the typical behavior of free markets." [1]

Rhea asserts that manipulation is possible in the day-to-day
movement of the averages, and said secondary reactions are
subject to such an influence to a more limited degree, but he
affirmed that the primary trend can never be manipulated. [2]

Hamilton asserted that a "limited number of stocks may be
manipulated at one time and may give an entirely false view of
the situation. It is impossible, however, to manipulate the
whole list so that the average price of [30] active stocks will
show changes sufficiently important to draw market deduc-
tions from them." [3]

Elsewhere, Hamilton states:

"Anybody will admit that while manipulation is possible in
the day-to-day market movement, and the short swing is sub-
ject to such an influence in a more limited degree, the great
market movement must be beyond the manipulation of the
combined financial interests of the world." [4]

He states further:

"...no power, not the U.S. Treasury and the Federal Reserve
System combined, could usefully manipulate forty active
stocks or deflect their accord to any but a negligible extent." [5]

Schabacker, while agreeing with Hamilton and Rhea that the
broad market is impervious to manipulation, states that it is possible for powerful insiders and major "market movers" to artifi-
cially create chart patterns in order to "trick" the technical analysts and profit thereby. He writes:

"Insiders and professional traders are by no means unaware of the growing public interest and education in chart theories and patterns. In normal trading there are certainly not enough chart traders to make it worthwhile for the professionals to play against them instead of against the general public, but we have learned that the professionals must play against someone in order to make their money. It is quite conceivable, therefore, that the insiders might take a 'crack' at chart traders now and then by manipulating false patterns in their company stocks, with the knowledge that by arranging certain chart pictures, they could draw in a certain amount of buying or selling, as they chose, with a view to strengthening their own position...

"The student's best defense, and his best policy in any case, is in keeping and watching a goodly number of individual charts. The professional can hardly swing more than a handful of his pet individual issues to suit himself, much less the market as a whole, and the misleading action of a few individual charts will often be adequately exposed by the contrary indications of a great many other ones.

"And then, of course, there is always available the protection of the stop loss order deserving situations which do not work out properly, as well as the inevitable development of new technical indications which help the student to revise his forecast and market position. It is reasonably safe to say that even the most powerful and well-balanced of operators cannot long prevent the chart's showing the true technical picture." [6]

As Schabacker points out, this form of manipulation, which is quite rare, can occur *only* in thinly-traded, lightly-held shares of stock with a very low number of shares outstanding.

As a rule, this type of stock should be avoided anyway since thinly traded stocks do not possess the requisite "human factor" to create the reliable chart patterns with forecasting value discussed in this book. When such patterns do form (or *appear* to form in such issues) they usually prove to be misleading anyway and cannot be relied upon. Even if they were reliable, an investor would want to avoid them if only because they are illiquid and therefore much more difficult to exit than actively traded issues. Thus, the chances of incurring financial losses in such shares are greatly increased.

A good "chartist" knows to stick only to those securities that are highly liquid and possess a sufficient amount of trading activity so as to make technical analysis worthwhile.

Notes

[1] Edwards & Magee, *Technical Analysis of Stock Trends*, Amacom, 1948, 1997, pg. 510-511
[2] Rhea, Robert, *The Dow Theory*, Fraser Publishing Co., 1993, pg. 16
[3] Ibid., pg. 129
[4] Ibid., pg. 134
[5] Ibid., pg. 201
[6] Schabacker, R.W., *Technical Analysis and Stock Market Profits*, Pitman Publishing, 1997 (originally published in 1932), pg. 426

Chapter 7

Support and Resistance

The concept of support and resistance in the charts is basic to the understanding of price patterns and their implications.

Edwards & Magee defined support as the "buying, actual or potential, sufficient in volume to halt a downtrend in prices for an appreciable period." [1] Resistance, of course, is the antithesis of this and consists of selling, actual or potential, in sufficient volume to keep prices from rising for a time. "Support and resistance, as thus defined, are nearly but not quite synonymous with demand and supply, respectively." [2]

Further expounding this concept, Edwards & Magee tell us:

"A support level is a price level at which sufficient demand for a stock appears to hold a downtrend temporarily at least, and possibly reverse it, i.e., start prices moving up again. A resistance zone by the same token, is a price level at which sufficient supply of a stock is forthcoming to stop, and possibly turn back, its uptrend. There is, theoretically, a certain amount of supply and a certain amount of demand at any given price level...But a support range represents a concentra-

Support and Resistance Levels

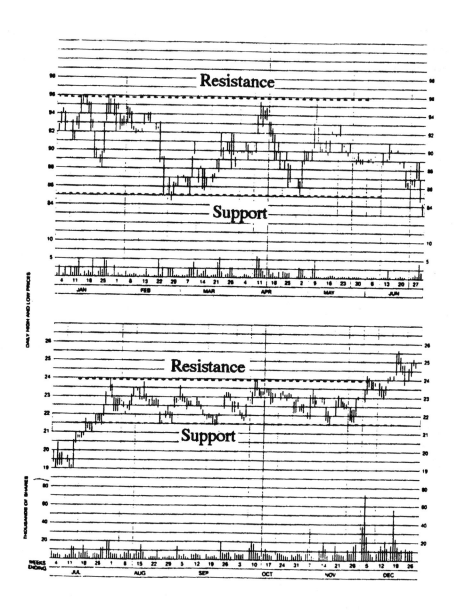

tion of demand, and a resistance range represents a concentration of supply." [3]

Support and resistance—in their basic forms—are represented on the charts as follows:

In a trending market, especially one in which prices travel within the confines of a clearly defined channel, the support and resistance lines will tend to keep prices within the boundaries. Thus, prices normally fluctuate within the channel, bouncing from support to resistance in an alternating "zigzag" pattern.

Support and resistance are more than just upward trending or downward trending channel lines. They may be encountered from a variety of chart patterns and other places of price congestion on the charts.

One rule of thumb for determining where a market or security will meet with either support or resistance on the charts is to find previous chart areas where consolidation has occurred. If, for example, a particular stock has stalled out in a net sideways or other congestion pattern at a certain level in the recent past before falling to a lower level, it is all but likely that the stock will encounter difficulty in penetrating that same level later on as it rallies and tries to overcome it. This, of course, does not necessarily mean that the former area of consolidation (in this case, resistance) will prove impenetrable; to the contrary, it will probably be overcome eventually. But not without considerable effort on behalf of the buyers. The greater the congestion, the greater the effort required to overcome that congestion, whether it is in the form of support or resistance. Thus, support and resistance serve as checks in the development of a trend (be it a rising or a falling trend) to keep the trend from moving too far, too fast and thus getting out of hand and eliciting violent reactions. (This does not apply, of course, in market crashes or "buying panics," in which case support and resistance levels become meaningless. But such instances are fortunately quite rare.

This leads us to the next related principle of support and resistance which Edwards & Magee elucidate for us:

"...here is the interesting and the important fact which, curiously enough, many casual chart observers appear never to grasp: These critical price levels constantly switch their roles from support to resistance and from resistance to support. A former top, once it has been surpassed, becomes a bottom zone in a subsequent downtrend; and an old bottom, once it has been penetrated, becomes a top zone in a later advancing phase." [4]

Thus, if a certain security breaks through an overhead resistance level at, say $50, then the moment prices are above the $50 level, it automatically becomes a support. Conversely, if the $50 in our hypothetical security had been a support checking prices from moving below it and the $50 level is suddenly penetrated then $50 automatically becomes resistance. This principle, which we will call the "principle of interchangeability," holds true for older levels of support and resistance as well, not just recent levels.

Other instances of support and resistance can be found not only in areas of chart congestion but in geometric chart patterns as well. The symmetrical triangle affords just such an example. Throughout the formation of the triangle, the upper and lower boundary lines serve as resistance and support, respectively. However, an even stronger level of support and resistance (depending on which direction prices take upon breaking out from the triangle) is provided by the apex of the triangle. By drawing a horizontal line from the apex and extending it across the chart an analyst will be provided with a reliable support/resistance level. However, such levels usually become weak as time passes. [5] Thus, a chartist will want to regard this as a strong support/resistance only in the days/weeks immediately following a price breakout from a triangle.

Concerning volume, it is sufficient merely to point out that the power of a resistance (or support) range is estimated by using the criterion of volume. [6] In other words, the greater the amount of volume that was recorded at the making of a top (resistance) or bottom (support) in a given market or security, the greater the strength of that top or bottom will be and the more effort will be necessary to penetrate it in the future. As Edwards & Magee put it:

"In brief, a single, sharp, high-volume bottom offers somewhat more resistance than a series of bottoms with the same volume spread out in time and with intervening rallies." [7]

Another criterion Edwards & Magee discuss that is worth noting here is the extent of the subsequent decline from a resistance zone. Or, to phrase it differently, how far will prices have to climb before they encounter the old bottom zone whose resistance potential the analyst attempts to appraise? "Generally speaking," Edwards & Magee write, "the greater the distance, the greater the resistance." [8]

In other words, the higher that prices must travel before breaking the previous top, the stronger the resistance that top is likely to hold.

Finally, in answer to the oft-asked question as to what exactly constitutes a legitimate "break" of either support or resistance, we would refer the analyst back to the old Edwards & Magee "three percent rule," which states that a break above a support or resistance level (or through a corresponding chart pattern) by distance of at least 3 percent, and accompanied by increased trading volume, should be viewed as the start of a new trend and therefore followed.

Notes

[1] Edwards & Magee, *Technical Analysis of Stock Trends*, Amacom, 1948, 1997, pg. 253
[2] Ibid., pg. 254
[3] Ibid., pg. 254
[4] Ibid., pg. 254-255
[5] Ibid., pg. 270
[6] Ibid., pg. 260
[7] Ibid., pg. 260
[8] Ibid., pg. 261

Chapter 8

Trendlines and Channels

O ne of the basic tenets of technical analysis is that prices move in trends. [1] Understanding this basic principle alone will give the technical analyst a major advantage over anyone using fundamental analysis.

There are only three types of trends a market may take: up, down, or sideways (horizontal). It remains up to the analyst to determine which of these three trends is in place at any given time. Admittedly, this is sometimes a difficult task since the primary, or major, trend may be up while prices may take a temporary downward path only to resume the previous uptrend once the "correction" is over. A major goal, then, of technical analysis is to determine price trends and identify turning points in the market.

How then are we to approach this task? The simplest and most effective way is through the use of trendlines, that is, a perfectly straight line drawn on the chart connecting either the bottoms (troughs) of prices in order to determine an uptrend, or the tops (peaks) of prices in order to determine a downtrend. As Edwards & Magee explain:

Trendlines and Channels

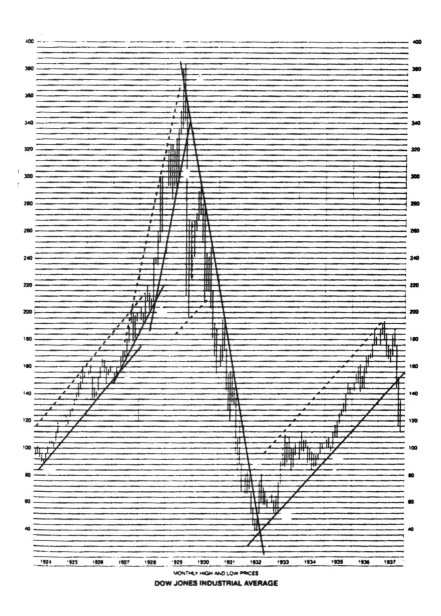

MONTHLY HIGH AND LOW PRICES
DOW JONES INDUSTRIAL AVERAGE

"If we actually apply a ruler to a number of charted price trends, we quickly discover that the line which most often is really straight in an uptrend is a line connecting the lower extremes of the minor recessions within those trends. On a descending price trend, the line most likely to be straight is the one that connects the tops of the minor rallies within it, while the minor bottoms may or may not fall along a straight edge. [2]

Trendlines, whether in the upward or downward slanting position, cannot be drawn arbitrarily but must correspond to a basic set of rules. One of these rules—given by Edwards & Magee—is that a straight line is mathematically determined by any two points along it:

"In order to draw a trendline, therefore, we require two determining points-two established top reversal points to fix a down trendline and two established bottom reversal points to fix an up trendline." [3]

One of the most useful purposes of a trendline is in establishing reversals or turning points in the trend. Reversals are indicated by a break below (or above, as the case may be) the trendline by at least 3 percent (the "three percent rule"). This must be strictly adhered to, for sometimes prices do break above or below a trendline only to recover and continue along the previously established trendline. A break of three percent or more, however, is very likely to represent a true turnaround of the trend.

Edwards & Magee give us two more useful rules for identifying turning points when using trendlines:

"1. When the trendline is broken (i.e., when prices drop down through it in decisive fashion), it signals that the advance has run out. It calls time for an intermediate-term trader to sell out that issue, and look for reinvestment opportunities elsewhere.

"2. When a small top reversal pattern [such as a head and shoulders, for instance] forms on the chart of an issue well up and away from that issue's intermediate up trendline, so that there apparently is room for the downside implications of the reversal formations to be carried out before the trendline is violated, then the intermediate-trend trader may well decide to ignore the small reversal pattern. He can hold on so long as the trendline holds." [4]

Of course, volume of trading activity (as with any technical measure or chart pattern) can and should be used to confirm the validity of a trendline breakthrough. As always, a noticeable increase in trading volume adds more weight to the legitimacy of any such trendline penetration. In fact, if a trendline penetration occurs on any given trading day on conspicuously high volume, even if the 3 percent rule has not been satisfied, it is often enough to qualify as a change of trend and the trader should respond accordingly. [5]

Edwards & Magee provide further tests which may be applied to judge the technical validity and the authority of an up trendline:

*"**A**. The greater the number of bottoms that have developed at (or very near) a trendline in the course of a series of minor up waves, the greater the importance of that line in the technical sense. With each successive 'test,' the significance of the line is increased...*

*"**B**. The length of the line, i.e., the longer it has held without being penetrated downside by prices, the greater its technical significance. This principle, however, requires some qualification . If your trendline is drawn from two original bottoms which are very close together in time-say, less than a week apart-it is subject to error; it may be too steep or (more often) too flat. If the latter, prices may move away from it and stay high above it for a long time, they may then turn down and have declined well along in an intermediate correction before the trendline thus drawn is reached. But if the*

trendline has been drawn from bottoms which are far enough apart to have developed as independent wave components of the trend you are trying to define, with a good rally and 'open water' between them, then it is more apt to be the true trendline. Greater weight should be given to the number of bottoms that have formed on a trendline (Test A) than to its length alone (Test B).

"C. The angle of the trendline (to the horizontal) is also, to some degree, a criterion of its validity as a true delimeter of intermediate trend...Steep lines are of little forecasting value to the technician. The flatter, more nearly horizontal the trendline, the more important it is technically, and, in consequence, the greater the significance of any downside break through it." [6]

Further expounding on the principle of the angle of the trendline, Edwards & Magee point out that intermediate uptrends on the daily charts, "in the great majority of issues selling in the 10 to 50 range, rise at an angle of approximately 30 degrees to the horizontal. Some will be a trifle flatter, some a trifle steeper, but it is surprising to see how often the trendline falls very close to the 30-degree slope in stocks of average volatility and activity. [7]

As a corollary to this, it must be pointed out that this applies only to charts made on semilogarithmic scale.

The Fan Principle

Secondary corrective trends (i.e., corrections retracing an amount less than 20 percent of the previous price movement) are common occurrences in any market. It remains, therefore, for the chartist to identify them, or more importantly, the end of a secondary correction and the beginning of the resumption of the primary trend.

To be expected, corrective patterns almost always take geometric forms that fall under the rubric of our craft. One such example is the fan principle, or simply "fan lines," as they are also known. Edwards & Magee explain:

"In a bull market, it starts with a sharp reaction which proceeds for several days-perhaps for as much as two weeks-producing a steep minor trendline. This line is broken upside by a quick minor rally, after which prices slide off again in a duller and less precipitate trend. A second minor trendline may now be drawn from the original high point across the top of the upthrust that broke the first trend. This second trendline is broken by another partial recovery thrust, and a third and still duller and flatter sell-off ensues. A third trendline can now be drawn from the original high across the top of the second upthrust. The whole move, by this time, has taken roughly and irregularly a 'saucering-out' form. The three trendlines drawn from the original reversal point from which the corrective decline started, each at a flatter angle than its predecessor, are known as fan lines. And the rule is that when the third fan line is broken upside, the low of the intermediate correction has been seen." [8]

The purpose, then, of the fan principle is to determine the end of intermediate reactions in a bull market and of intermediate recoveries in a bear market. [9]

Fan Lines

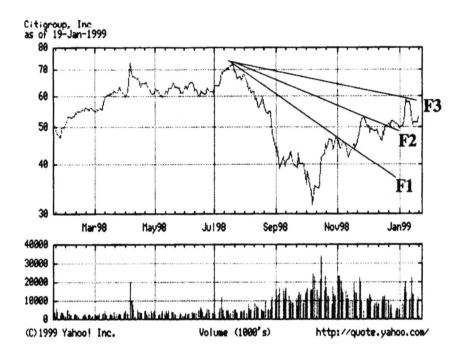

Channels

Finally, we will discuss a trendline formation most common in actively traded securities of large outstanding issues (and least often in the less popular and the relatively thinly traded equities which receive only sporadic attention from investors)-channels. Edwards & Magee define a channel thusly:

"In a fair share of normal trends...the minor waves are sufficiently regular to be defined at their other extremes by another line. That is, tops of the rallies composing an intermediate advance sometimes develop along a line which is approximately parallel to the basic trendline projected along their bottoms. This parallel might be called the return line, since it marks the zone where reactions (return moves against the prevailing trend) originate. The area between basic trendline and return line is the trend channel." [10]

Prices bounded by trend channels follow the rule of alternation in which a move that meets with the top of the channel line elicits a bounce to the bottom line, and vice-versa in a repeating pattern.

Notes

[1] Edwards & Magee, *Technical Analysis of Stock Trends*, Amacom, 1948, 1997, pg. 282
[2] Ibid., pg. 283-284
[3] Ibid., pg. 284-285
[4] Ibid., pg. 289
[5] Ibid., pg. 296
[6] Ibid., pg. 291-292
[7] Ibid., pg. 293
[8] Ibid., pg. 313
[9] Ibid., pg. 314
[10] Ibid., pg. 302

Chapter 9

One-Day Reversals

Our study of technical analysis would not be complete without an examination of chart phenomena which often provide the analyst with valuable warnings of turning points in the trend. While this particular branch of trend reversal analysis falls outside the rubric of classical Western technical analysis, it is a staple of Japanese chart analysis and has proven to be worthy of attention by every serious student of technical analysis.

These reversal patterns, which we label "one-day reversals," are among the easiest of all chart patterns to spot because they encompass only one day's record on the bar chart. (Of course, these patterns are also valid on weekly bar charts and forecast reversals of even greater significance). In Japanese technical analysis there exists an entire discipline dedicated to this subject—known as candlestick analysis—but we do not address the subject here. What we are here examining is much simpler and often has greater forecasting significance. And unlike a great many of the chart patterns we have previously discussed, these one-day reversals are accurate in their forecasting implications nearly every single time they appear in the charts.

Key Reversals

Key reversal day

Key reversal day

The first one-day reversal in the charts we'll look at is known as the "key reversal." In an uptrend, it consists of a trading session in which prices have made a new intraday high—often a significantly higher level than the previous trading day—only to reverse lower and close below the previous day's close.

It is so named "key reversal" because it resembles a skeleton key in appearance on the bar chart.

In a downtrend just the opposite is true of a key reversal-a move to a new low during a trading session only to see prices close above the previous day's close. Both of these phenomena signal an immediate reversal of trend.

Closing High/Low Reversals

Closing low

Closing high

Whenever these patterns appear on the charts they should be duly noted and acted upon immediately as their forecasting reliability is extremely high.

Another one-day reversal phenomenon with similar forecasting reliability is what is known in Japanese candlestick analysis as either a "shooting star" or a "gravestone doji" or "dragonfly doji." Since we are dealing with traditional Western bar charts (consisting of the day's high, low and close) we have taken the liberty of renaming them "closing high" and "closing low" reversal patterns depending on which direction the market is taking at their appearance. They are both similar to the key reversal patterns in that they usually (but not always) make intraday highs or lows only to reverse and close at the extreme low point of the trading day. Unlike key reversals, however, they do not have to close above or below (depending on the direction of the market trend) the previous day's close to have validity. For instance, in an upward trending market, a closing low reversal (signaling a reversal lower) could be given by a bar in which prices close on the extreme low of the day, but above the previous day's close. All that is necessary to verify its forecasting significance is the length of the bar, which must be of reasonable length.

It must be emphasized that while closing high and closing low reversals reliably forecast changes of trend, and therefore constitute an important facet of turning point analysis, they do not forecast amplitude or duration of trend—only that there will be some type of reversal in the direction prices take. Unlike the other chart patterns discussed in this book, there is no measuring formula for one-day reversal patterns.

Tweezers Top and Bottom Reversals

Tweezers top

Tweezers bottom

Finally, another pattern that serves advance notice of a change in trend but is not technically a one-day reversal but a "two-day" reversal is the "tweezers top" pattern. This pattern, also based on Japanese candlestick analysis, occurs when two consecutive trading days on the bar chart produce two identical high points for the day. The market does not necessarily have to close at those intraday high points (although it can), but the two extreme high points for the two back-to-back trading sessions as shown by the upper end of the bars must be identical to one another. Unlike the key reversal, the tweezers top rarely forecasts a major change in trend, only a minor or intermediate change, and it is not uncommon for the market to retrace as much as one-third of its previous gains on the appearance of this pattern. The opposite of the tweezers top, of course, is the tweezers bottom, which acts the same as the tweezers top, only in reverse.

While these above mentioned patterns are by no means everyday occurrences, keeping an open eye out for them will greatly enhance the analyst's ability in spotting turning points in advance of an actual change in market trend and will therefore serve as a complement to basic chart pattern and technical analysis.

Chapter 10

Conclusion

While this book by no means represents a detailed and comprehensive overview of technical analysis, it is the author's intention that it presents the basics of this excellent craft in a manner both concise and readily comprehended by both laymen and professionals alike. For the neophyte, this work should be read as a foundational work to the wide and extremely diverse world of technical analysis-an instruction manual containing all the most useful and basic elements of chart pattern analysis as well as a stimulant to further learning. For the professional, this book should serve as a useful reference for "brushing up on the basics," something which even the best and most experienced of analysts must do from time to time.

It is further hoped that by reading this book, investors and analysts alike will gain a deeper understanding of the inexorable forces which govern free markets everywhere-forces that while unseen, can be recognized and used for profit through the tool of technical analysis. It must not be supposed, however, that technical analysis in the hands of an investor is a "crystal ball." This is where most students of technical analysis become frustrated and discouraged and are apt to conclude that technical analysis is of no value: it is because they treat it as a means of knowing the future. This is a grave error and one to be avoided at all costs. It is not a crystal ball, but rather a method whereby the skilled analyst might improve his trading and, most importantly, avoid unnecessary losses. More than anything else, technical analysis is a risk management tool, to use the modern vernacular. When properly applied, it affords the trader or investor the advantage of being able to recognize and profit from various market trends and avoid profit losses. This is the real utility of technical analysis-not in its seeming ability to forecast the future. Sometimes, it does indeed accurately forecast the future, but not frequently enough to be labeled as reliable.

It is this author's observation that applying the principles discussed in this book will result in an accurate reading of the market roughly 75 percent of the time. It is up to the analyst to fill that additional 25 percent gap with a combination of an analysis of present business conditions and outlook (i.e., fundamental analysis), acquired market intuition (derived from years of trading experience), and a little good luck thrown in for good measure. This is the reality of trading and investing, but even this is a thousand times greater than trying to make money in the markets without the aid of some form of market analysis.

The bottom line is that there is no way of beating the market 100 percent of the time. But for as long as free markets exist, the trader has at his disposal a most wondrous and profitable means of coming out ahead in his dealings through pure and simple technical analysis.

Chapter 11

Dictionary of Terms

Accumulation

The first phase of a bull market. The period in which far-sighted investors begin to buy shares from discouraged or distressed sellers. Financial reports are usually at their worst and the public is completely disgusted with the stock market. Volume is only moderate but beginning to increase on the rallies.

Accumulation/Distribution

Momentum indicator that associates changes in price and volume. The indicator is based on the premise that the higher the volume that accompanies a price move, the more significant the price move.

Advance/Decline line

The advance/decline line is undoubtedly the most widely-used measurement of market breadth. It is a cumulative total of the advancing/declining issues. When compared to the movement of the market index, the A/D line has proven to be an effective gauge of the stock market's strength. The A/D line has to confirm the market movements.

The A/D line is calculated by subtracting the number of stocks that declined in price for the day from the number of stocks that advanced, and then adding this value to a cumulative total.

Advisory services

Privately circulated publications that comment upon the future course of financial markets and for which a subscription is usually required.

Evidence suggests that the advisory services in aggregate act in a manner completely opposite to that of the majority and therefore represent a indicator of a contrarian opinion. Advisory Sentiment Index = percentage of bullish market newsletter writers in relation to the total of all those expressing an opinion.

Amplitude of cycle

Normally the amplitude of a cycle is a function of its duration; i.e. the longer the cycle the bigger the swing.

Arithmetic scale

All units of measure on an arithmetic scale are plotted using the same vertical distance so that the difference in space between 2 and 4 is the same as that between 20 and 22. This scale is not particularly satisfactory for long-term price movements, since a rise from 2 to 4 represents a doubling of the price whereas a rise from 20 to 22 represents only a 10% increase.

Bear market

Period in which there is essentially a long decline in prices interrupted by important rallies, usually for a long time. Bear markets generally consist of three phases. The first phase is distribution, the second is panic and the third is akin to a washout. Those investors who have held on through the first two phases finally give up during the third phase and liquidate.

Bear spreading

The short sale of a future or option of a nearby month and the purchase of a distant contract. (One notable exception to this principle in the traditional commodity markets is the precious metals group. Bull and bear markets in gold, silver and platinum are led by the distant months.)

Bear trap

Corrections in a bear market which, can easily be confused with a reversal or a new bull market. If you are not careful, you can be washed out by a bear trap.

This signal can also suggest that the rising trend of an index or stock has reversed, but which proves to be false.

Bull market

A period in which prices are primarily rising, normally for an extended period. Usually, but not always, divisible into three phases. The first phase is accumulation. The second phase is one of a fairly steady advance with increasing volume. The third phase is marked by considerable activity as the public begins to recognize and attempt to profit from the rising market.

Bull trap

A signal which suggests that the declining trend of an index or stock has reversed, but which proves to be false.

Bull spreading

The purchase of a nearby futures/options contract and a short sale of a distant contract. In certain types of bull markets which are caused by a tightness in the supply/demand situation, the nearby contract months usually rise faster than the distant ones.

Beta

Measurement of sensitivity to market movements. The trading cycle (four weeks) breaks down in two shorter alpha and beta cycles, with an average of two weeks each (Walt Bressert).

Blow-offs (Climatic top)

A sharp advance accompanied by extraordinary volume; i.e. a much larger volume than the normal increase which signals the final "blow-off" of the trend. This is followed either by a reversal (or at least a period of stagnation, formation or consolidation) or by a correction.

Bond market sector

The bond market (i.e. the long end) has three main sectors, which are classified according to issuer.

- US government
- Tax-exempt issuers (i.e. state and local governments)
- Corporate issuers

Breadth (Market)

Breadth relates to the number of issues participating in a move. A rally is considered suspect if the number of advancing issues diminishes as the rally develops. Conversely, if a decline is associated with increasingly fewer falling stocks, it is considered to be a bullish sign.

Breakaway gap

The hole or gap in the chart which is created when a stock or commodity breaks out of an area pattern (areas on the bar chart where no trading has taken place). This gap usually occurs at the completion of an important price pattern and usually signals the beginning of a significant market move.

Breakaway gaps usually occur on heavy volume. More often than not, breakaway gaps are not filled.

Breakout

When a stock or commodity exits an area pattern.

Buying pressure

Buying or selling pressure is measured by volume indicators. It measures the strength of the buying or selling.

Call options

Options which give the buyer the right to buy the underlying contract or stock at a specific price within a certain period and which oblige the seller to sell the contract or stock for the premium received before the expiration of the designated time period.

Cash index

Index expressed in money. This is in contrast to futures prices.

Channel lines

The channel line, or the return line as it is sometimes called, is a line parallel to the basic trend line. It is the line in a bull market drawn parallel to the basic uptrend line which connects the lows.

Coils

Another word for a symmetrical triangle. A symmetrical triangle is composed of a series of two or more rallies and reactions in which each succeeding peak is lower than its predecessor, and the bottom of each succeeding reaction is higher than its predecessor.

Commodity options

A commodity gives the holder the right, but not the obligation, to purchase (a call) or sell (a put) on an underlying futures contract at a specific price within a specific period of time.

Composite average

A stock average comprised of the stocks which make up the Dow Jones Industrial Average (DJIA) and the Dow Jones Utility Average.

Composite market index

Basically a market index composed of a selection of specific stocks.

Confirmation

In a pattern the confirmation is the point at which a stock or commodity exits an area pattern in the expected direction by an amount of price and volume sufficient to meet minimum pattern requirements for a bona fide breakout. This is also true for oscillators. To confirm a new high or a new low in a stock or commodity, an oscillator needs to reach a new high or low as well. Failure of the oscillator to confirm a new high or a new low is called divergence and would be considered an early indication of a potential reversal in direction.

Congestion area

The sideways trading area from which area patterns evolve. Not all congestion periods produce a recognizable pattern however.

Consolidation

Also called a continuation pattern, it is an area pattern which breaks out in the direction of the previous trend.

Contrary opinion

A measure of sentiment is useful in assessing the majority view, from which a contrary opinion can be derived.

Cycles

The prices of many commodities reflect seasonal cycles. Due to the agricultural nature of most commodities, these cycles are easily explained and understood. However, for securities the cyclical nature is more difficult to explain. Human nature is probably responsible.

Decennial pattern

A pattern first cited by Edgar Lawrence Smith. It is a ten-year pattern, or cycle of stock price movements, which has essentially repeated itself over a 58-year period.

The decennial pattern can be of greater value if it is used to identify where the strong and weak points usually occur and then to check whether other technical phenomena are consistent.

Diffusion index

A diffusion index shows the percentage of indicators which are above their corresponding levels in a previous period (in this case six months earlier). The indicators are the coincident economic indicators which tend to rise and fall coincidentally with the overall economy. These indicators thus provide a good approximation of the economy. For example: industrial production, consumer installment debt, the federal budget deficit and inflation.

Discount rate

The discount rate is the rate at which banks can borrow directly from the Fed. The Fed can reduce bank reserves by raising the discount rate and expand reserves by lowering the discount rate. In practice the discount rate has little actual influence on interest rates.

Distribution

The first phase of a bear market. During this first phase far-sighted investors sense the fact that business earnings have reached an abnormal height and unload their holdings at an increasing pace (accumulation).

Divergence

Divergence refers to a situation in which different delivery months, related markets or technical indicators fail to confirm one another. Divergence is a valuable concept in market analysis and one of the best early warning signals for impending trend reversals.

Diversification

Limiting risk exposure by spreading the investments over different markets or instruments. The more negative the correlation between the markets, the more diversified the risk.

Dominant cycle

Dominant cycles continuously affect futures prices and can be clearly identified. These cycles are the only ones of real value for forecasting purposes. Most futures markets have at least five dominant cycles.

Long-term cycle ―――――> two or more years in length

Seasonal cycle ―――――> one year

Primary or intermediate cycle―――――> 9 to 26 weeks

Trading cycle―――――> four weeks

Short-term cycle―――――> several hours to several days

Dow theory

In 1897 Charles Dow developed two broad market averages. The industrial average included 12 blue-chip stocks and the rail average was comprised of 20 railroad enterprises. The Dow theory resulted from a series of articles published by Charles Dow in the Wall Street Journal between 1900 and 1902. The Dow theory is the forerunner to most principles of modern technical analysis.

Basic tenets of the Dow theory:

- the averages discount everything;
- the market has three trends: primary, secondary and minor
- major trends have three phases;
- the averages must confirm each other;
- volume must confirm the trend (volume must expand in the direction of the major trend);
- a trend is assumed to be in effect until it gives definite signals that it has reversed.

Downtrend

The trend is simply the direction of the market. A downtrend is a trend which is marked by descending peaks and troughs; in other words, lower subsequent highs and lower lows. An uptrend would be defined as a series of successively higher peaks and troughs (higher highs and higher lows).

Elliot Wave

Theory of market behavior by R.N. Elliot.

Basic tenets of the Elliot Wave principle:

- pattern, ratio and time in that order of importance;
- pattern refers to the wave patterns or formations that comprise one of the most important elements of the theory;
- ratio analysis is useful for determining retracement points and price objectives by measuring the relationship between the different waves;
- and time is used to confirm wave patterns and ratios.

Basic concepts Elliot Wave principle:

- action is followed by reaction;
- there are five waves in the direction of the main trend, followed by three corrective waves;
- a 5-3 move completes a cycle. The 5-3 move then becomes two subdivisions of the next higher 5-3 wave; and
- the underlying 5-3 pattern remains constant although the time span of each may vary.
- objectives by measuring the relationship between the different waves; and time is used to confirm wave patterns and ratios.

Envelopes

An envelope is comprised of two moving averages. One moving average is shifted upward and the second moving average is shifted downward. Envelopes define the upper and lower boundaries of a stock's normal trading range.

Exhaustion gap

The gap that appears near the end of a market move. Towards the end of an uptrend, prices leap forward with a final gasp.

However, this forward leap quickly loses ground and prices decrease within a couple of days or a week. When prices close under this last gap, it is usually a clear indication that the exhaustion gap has made its appearance. This is a classic example of when the filling of a gap in an uptrend has very bearish implications.

Exponential smoothing

The exponentially smoothed average assigns a greater weight to the more recent activity. It is therefore a weighted moving average. Mathematically, a single exponential smoothing is calculated as follows:

- $X = (C-X_p)K+X_p$

- X is exponential smoothing for the current period.

- C is closing price for the current period.

- X_p is exponential smoothing for the previous period.

- K is smoothing constant, equal to $2/n + 1$ for Compu Trac and $2/n$ for Back Trac.

- n is total number of periods in a simple moving average, which is roughly approximated by X.

Failures

Normally, a failure is when a completed pattern is not confirmed by the direction of the following move. The failure (in the Elliot Wave) shows a situation in which, in a bull market for example, wave 5 breaks down into the required five waves, but fails to exceed the top of wave 3.

Fan lines

Fan lines are constructed as follows:

Two extreme points are identified on the chart, usually an important top and bottom. A vertical line is then drawn from the second extreme to the beginning of the move. This vertical line is then divided by 38%, 50% and 62%, with lines drawn through each point from the beginning of the trend. These three lines should function as support and resistance points on subsequent reactions by measuring 38%, 50% and 62% Fibonacci retracements.

Fibonacci numbers

A number sequence rediscovered by Fibonacci. In Liber Abaci, the Fibonacci sequence is first presented as a solution to a mathematical problem involving the reproduction rate of rabbits. The number sequence presented is 1, 1, 2, 3, 5, 8, 13, 21, 34, 55, 114 and so on to infinity.

In technical analysis, the Fibonacci numbers are used to predict or measure future moves in stocks or to predict retracement levels.

Filter rules

The rule for confirming a breakthrough or a breakout. An example of a filter rule is the 3% penetration criterion. This price filter is used mainly for breaking off longer-term trend lines, but requires that the trend line be broken on a closing basis by at least 3%. The 3% rule does not apply to some financial futures, such as the interest rate markets.

Another example is a time filter, such as the two-day rule.

Flags (contnuation pattern)

A flag looks like a flag on the chart. That is, it looks like a flag if it appears in an uptrend. The picture is naturally upside down in a downtrend. It might be described as a small, compact parallelogram of price fluctuations, or a tilted rectangle which slopes back moderately against the prevailing trend.

Flow of funds

Flow of funds analysis refers to the cash position of the different groups, such as mutual funds or large institutional accounts. The thinking here is that the larger the cash position, the more funds available for stock purchases. While these forms of analysis are generally considered to be of secondary importance, it often seems that stock market technicians place more reliance on them than on traditional market analysis.

Gann angles

Gann divided price actions into eighths: 1/8, 2/8, ... 8/8. He also divided price actions into
thirds: 1/3 and 2/3:

1/8 = 12.5%
2/8 = 25.0%
1/3 = 33.0%
3/8 = 37.5%
4/8 = 50.0%
5/8 = 62.5%
2/3 = 67.0%
6/8 = 75.0%
7/8 = 87.5%
8/8 = 100.0%

The 50% retracement is the most important to Gann. Gann believed that the other percentages were also present in market action, but with diminishing importance.

Gaps

Gaps are simply areas on the bar chart where no trading has taken place. In an uptrend, for example, prices open above the highest price of the previous day, leaving a gap or open space on a chart which is not filled during the day. In a downtrend, the day's highest price is below the previous day's low.

Upside gaps are signs of market strength, while downside gaps are usually signs of weakness.

Group rotation

The overall market consists of many stock groups which are a reflection of the companies making up the various segments of the economy. The economy, defined by an aggregate measure such as Gross National Product (GNP), is either rising or falling at any given time. However, there are very few periods in which all segments are advancing or declining simultaneously. This is because the economy is not one homogeneous unit. Group rotation is the rotation within the different groups of stocks depending on at which stage the economic cycle is at the moment.

Hedging

To obviate risk and avoid speculation. Futures and options can be used for hedging.

High-low indicator

The new high-low cumulative indicator is a long-term market momentum indicator. It is a cumulative total of the difference between the number of stocks reaching a new 52-week high and the number of stocks reaching a new 52-week low. This indicator provides a confirmation of the current trend. Most of the time the indicator will move in the same direction as the major market indices. However, when the indicator and market move in opposite directions (divergence), the market is likely to reverse.

Insiders

Any person who directly or indirectly owns more than 10% of any class of stock listed on a national exchange, or who is an officer or director of the company in question.

Intermediate trend

An intermediate, or secondary, trend is the direction of the trend in a period from three weeks to as many months.

Intra-day

A record of price data during the day, such as 15-minute bar charts. These intra-day charts are extremely important for the timing aspects of trading.

Key reversal day

The term "key reversal day" is widely misunderstood. All one-day reversals are potential key reversal days, but only a few actually become key reversal days. Many of the one-day reversals represent nothing more than temporary pauses in the existing trend after which the trend resumes its course. The true key reversal day marks an important turning point, but it cannot be correctly identified as such until well after the fact; that is, not until after prices have moved significantly in the opposite direction from the prior trend.

Kondratieff cycle

The Kondratieff wave, a 54-year cycle, is named after a Russian economist. This is a long-term cycle identified in prices and economic activity. Since the cycle is extremely long term, it has repeated itself only three times in the stock market.

The up-wave is characterized by rising prices, a growing economy and mildly bullish stock markets. The plateau is characterized by stable prices, peak economic capacity and strong bullish stock markets. The down-wave is characterized by falling prices, severe bear markets and often a major war.

Limit move

A move limited by the uptick or downtick rule in commodity trading.

Log scale

Prices plotted on ratio or log scales show equal distances for similar percentage moves. For example, a move from 10 to 20 (a 100% increase) would be the same distance on a log chart as a move from 20 to 40 or 40 to 80.

Long-term cycle

A long-term cycle is basically two or more years in length.

Major market trend

The major market trend is the primary direction of the market. The Dow theory classifies the major trend as being in effect for longer than a year. Futures traders would be inclined to shorten the major trend to anything longer than six months.

Margin

This occurs when an investor pays part of the purchase price for a security and borrows the balance, usually from a broker; the margin is the difference between the market value of the stock and the loan which is made against it.

Margin: commodities versus stocks

The most important difference between stocks and commodity futures is the lower margin requirements on stock futures. All futures are traded at a margin, which is usually less than 10% of the value of the contract. The result of these low margin requirements is tremendous leverage. Relatively small price moves in either direction tend to be magnified according to their impact on overall trading results.

Margin debt
Debt caused by margin requirements.

Market averages

In stock market analysis, the starting point of all market analysis is always the broad market averages, such as the Dow Jones Average or the Standard & Poor's 500 Index. A market average is usually an index of the most important stocks in the market or a broad market index that covers 98-99% of the market as a whole.

Member short sale ratio

The member short ratio (MSR) is a market sentiment indicator which measures the short selling activity of the members of the New York Stock Exchange. "Members" trade on the floor of the exchange, either on their own behalf or for their clients. Knowing what the "smart money" is doing is often a good indication of the near-term market direction.

The MSR is the inverse of the Public Short Sale Ratio.

Minor market trend

The minor, or near-term, trend usually lasts less than three weeks and represents shorter-term fluctuations in the intermediate trend.

Momentum indicator

The momentum indicator measures the amount a security's price has changed over a given time span. It displays the rate of change as a ratio.

Most active stocks

The most active stocks are stocks that are traded the most over a certain period. Statistics on the most active stocks are published in the general press on both a daily and weekly basis. Usually the 20 most active stocks are recorded.

Moving average

A moving average is the average of the closing prices of x periods added up and divided by x. The term "moving" is used because the calculation moves forward in time. Moving averages are used to help identify the different kinds of trends (short-term, intermediate medium, etc.).

A smoothing device with a time lag.

The moving average is one of the most versatile and widely used of all technical indicators. Because of the way it is constructed and the fact that it can be so easily quantified and tested, it is also used as a smoothing device to isolate a trend. It is, therefore, the basis for most mechanical trend-following systems in use today.

Moving average crossovers

One method used by technicians in terms of moving averages. A buy signal is produced when the shorter average crosses above the longer-term moving average. Two popular combinations are the 5- and 20-day averages and the 10- and 40-day averages.

Neckline

Support or resistance level in a Head & Shoulders pattern. The neckline connects the lows or highs of the "shoulders" depending on the situation (H & S bottom or top formation).

Nominality

The principle of nominality is based on the premise that, despite the differences that exist in the various markets and allowing for some variation in implementing cyclical principles, there seems to be a set of harmonically related cycles that affect all markets. A nominal model of cycle lengths can be used as a starting point for any market.

Odd-lot ratios

There are a few odd-lot ratios:
• Odd-lot balance index (OLBI)
• Odd-lot short ratio
• Odd-lot purchases/sales

The OLBI is a market sentiment indicator that shows the ratio of odd-lot sales to purchases (an "odd-lot" is a stock transaction of less than 100 shares). The assumption is that "odd-lotters", the market's smallest traders, do not know what they are doing.

When the odd-lot balance index is high, odd-lotters are selling more than they are buying and are therefore bearish on the market. To trade contrarily to the odd-lotters, you should buy when they are selling.

On-balance volume

On-balance volume (OBV) is a momentum indicator that relates volume to price. The OBV is a running total of volume. It shows whether volume is flowing into or out of a security. When the security closes higher than the previous close, all of the day's volume is considered up-volume. When the security closes lower than the previous close, all of the day's volume is considered down-volume.

The basic assumption in OBV analysis is that OBV changes precede price changes. The theory is that smart money can be seen as flowing into a security by a rising OBV. When the public then moves into a security, both the security and the OBV will surge ahead.

Open interest

Open interest is the number of open contracts of a given futures or options contract. An open contract can be a long or short open contract that has not been exercised, or has been closed out or allowed to expire. Open interest is really more a data field than an indicator.

Oscillators

Method of creating an indicator. The oscillator is extremely useful in non-trending markets where prices fluctuate in a horizontal price band, or trading range, creating a market situation in which most trend-following systems simply do not work that well.

The three most important uses for the oscillator

- The oscillator is most useful when its value reaches an extreme reading near the upper or lower end of its bound aries. The market is said to be over bought when it is near the upper extreme and oversold when it is near the lower extreme. This warns that the price trend is overextended and vulnerable;
- A divergence between the oscillator and the price action, when the oscillator is in an extreme position, is usually an important warning signal; and
- Crossing the zero line can give important trading signals in the direction of the price trend.

Overbought level

An opinion on the price level. It may refer to a specific indicator or to the market as a whole after a period of vigorous buying, after which it may be argued that prices are overextended for the time being and are in need of a period of downward or horizontal adjustment.

Oversold level

An opinion on the price level. A price move that has overextended itself on the downside.

Overowned stocks

A stock is overowned when fashion-conscious investors are all interested in buying a certain stock.

Point & Figure

Method of charting prices. A new plot on a P&F chart is made only when the price changes by a given amount. P&F charts are only concerned with measuring price.

P&F charts are constructed using combinations of X's and 0's known as "boxes". The X shows that prices are moving up, the 0 that they are moving down. The size of the box and the amount of the reversal are important.

Primary trend

This is the most important long-term trend. A primary trend usually consists of five intermediate trends. Three of the trends form part of the prevailing trend while the remaining two run counter to that trend.

Public/specialist short sale ratio

It measures the round-lot short selling by the public against the New York Stock Exchange specialists on the floor of the Exchange. It pits the smart money against one of the least informed categories of market participants.

Rally

A brisk rise following a decline or consolidation of the general price level of the market.

Reaction

A temporary price weakness following an upswing.

Relative strength (RS)

An RS line or index is calculated by dividing one price by another. Usually the divisor is a measure of "the market", such as the DJIA or the Commodity Research Bureau (CRB) Index. A rising line indicates that the index or stock is performing better than "the market" and vice versa. Trends in the RS can be monitored by moving average crossovers, trend line breaks, etc. in the same way as any other indicator.

Resistance

Resistance is the opposite of support and represents a price level or area over the market where selling pressure overcomes buying pressure and a price advance is turned back. A resistance level is usually identified by a previous peak.

Retracement

Retracements are basically countertrend moves. After a particular market move, prices retrace a portion of the previous trend before resuming the move in the original direction. These countertrend moves tend to fall into certain predictable percentage parameters. The best known application of this phenomenon is the 50% retracement. For example: a market is trending higher and travels from the 100 level to the 200 level. The subsequent reaction very often retraces about half of the prior move.

Seasonal cycle

Seasonal cycles are cycles caused by the seasonal changes in the supply-demand relationship (caused by factors that occur at about the same time every year).

Secondary trend

Secondary trends are corrections in the primary trend and usually consist of shorter waves that would be identified as near-term dips and rallies.

Sentiment indicator

Indicators that measure the market sentiment, such as:

- Specialist Public Ratio
- Short Interest Ratio
- Insider Trading
- Advisory Services

Short interest

The short interest is a figure published around the end of the month citing the number of shares that have been sold short on the NYSE.

Speed resistance lines

Technique that combines the trend line with percentage retracements. The speed resistance lines measure the rate of a trend's ascent or descent (in other words, its speed).

Stock index futures

Futures contract on indices.

Support area

Support is a level or area on the chart under the market where buying interest is sufficiently strong to overcome selling pressure. As a result, a decline is halted and prices turn back up again. A support level is usually identified beforehand by a previous reaction low.

Trend line

A trend line is a straight line drawn up to the right that connects important points in a chart. An up trend line is a line that connects the successive reaction lows, and a down trend line connects the successive rally peaks.

Upside/Downside volume

Measurements of upside/downside volume try to separate the volume into advancing and declining stocks. By using this technique, it can be subtly determined whether accumulation or distribution is taking place.

Volume

Volume represents the total amount of trading activity in that market or stock over a given period.

Whipsaws

Misleading moves or breakouts.

Chapter 12
Bibliography

Achelis, Steven B., *Technical Analysis From A to Z*, McGraw Hill, 1995.

Apostolou, Nick and Barbara, *Keys to Investing in Common Stocks, Barron's,* 1995.

Edwards & Magee, *Technical Analysis of Stock Trends,* Amacom, 1948, 1997.

Fosback, Norman G., *Stock Market Logic*, Dearborn Financial Publishing, 1976, 1993.

Lefevre, Edwin, *Reminiscences of a Stock Operator,* John Wiley & Sons, Inc. 1995.

Prechter, Robert, *Prechter's Perspective*, New Classics Library, 1996

Pring, Martin, *Technical Analysis Explained*, McGraw-Hill, 1990, 1994.

Rhea, Robert, *The Dow Theory*, Fraser Publishing Co., 1993.

Schabacker, R.W., *Technical Analysis and Stock Market Profits*, Pitman Publishing, 1997 (originally published in 1932).

Chapter 13
Investment
Resource Guide

Tools for
Investment Success

SUGGESTED READING LIST

Technical Analysis From A to Z
by Steven B. Achelis

The creator of the most used Technical Analysis software in the world explains virtually every technical indicator known—over 120—with full descriptions and specific uses of each. On the practical use of technical analysis you won't find a more thorough or affordable work. "An essential addition to any technical library," says John Bollinger, former CNBC host.
$29.95 Item #T170x-2396

The Stock Market Barometer
by William P. Hamilton

Dow Theory Method—often known as the Stock Market Barometer—consistently remains a predictable strategy for forecasting the market. Now, this 1922 classic by the former Wall St. Journal editor, has been reissued with a fascinating new foreword. See how applicable this theory is to predicting—and profiting—from the markets today.
$19.95 Item #T170x-8443

The Dow Theory
by Robert Rhea

This is an explanation of Dow Theory development and an attempt to define its usefulness as an aid to speculation. Rhea carefully studied 252 editorials of Dow and Hamilton in order to present Dow Theory in terms that would be useful for the individual investor.
$17.00 Item #T170x-11108

Reminiscences of a Stock Operator
Edwin Lefevre

Generations of investors have benefited from this 1923 master-piece. Jack Schwager's new introduction explains why this account of Jesse Livermore, one of the greatest speculators ever—continues to be the most widely read book by the trading community. See why industry insider Martin Zweig says, "I keep a supply for people who come to work for me."
$19.95 Item #T170x-2116

Technical Analysis Explained, 3rd edition
by Martin Pring

Covers every aspect of technical analysis. Teaches you to interpret market cycles and select the best performing investments. Pring's classic text covers bar chart basics, moving averages, price patterns, RSI, stochastics and more—to help you build winning portfolios.
$49.95 Item #T170x-2373

Technical Analysis & Stock Market Profits
by R.W. Schabacker

Everyone from Edwards & Magee on consider this classic the foundation on which all technical analysis is built. It examines patterns, formations, trends, support and resistance areas, etc—which comprise the basis of modern technical analysis, from the Grandfather of it all, & the former finance editor at *Forbes* and the *New York Times*.
$65.00 Item #T170x-8473

Keys to Investing in Common Stocks
by Nick & Barbara Apostolou

Provides the latest information on stocks, clear explanations for the small investor, advice on dealing with a broker, when to buy, when to sell, how to develop a sound investment program, how to buy or sell over-the-counter stocks, how to do research before investing, how to recognize growth stocks versus speculative stocks, and much more.
$4.95 Item #T170x-10623

Technical Analysis of Stock Trends, 7th edition
by Edwards & Magee

A universally acclaimed classic, updated with the latest data in market performance and trends, on which the foundation of all technical analysis is built. Step-by-step coverage thoroughly explains and applies the current data. Stochastics, trend lines, stops, reversals, support/resistance and tactical usage of each.
$75.00 Item #T170x-2376

Martin Pring's Introduction to Technical Analysis
A CD-rom Seminar and Workbook
By Martin Pring

The foremost expert on technical analysis and forecasting financial markets gives you a one-on-one course in every aspect of technical analysis. This interactive guide explains how to evaluate trends, highs and lows, price/volume relationships, price patterns, moving averages and momentum indicators. The CD-rom includes videos, animated diagrams, audio clips and interactive tests. It's the user-friendly way to master technical analysis from an industry icon.
$49.95 Item #T170x-8521

Stock Market Logic
Norman G. Fosback

Offers comprehensive coverage of the stock market for investors and professionals, and presents a coherent philosophy, showing how investors with reasonable objectives can use this approach to reap steady rewards. Includes discussions on market indicators, econometrics and the market and stock selection theories. It outlines a financial management system to measure the market and keep score, and explains how to use market logic and mutual funds to maximize profit and reduce risk.
$30.00 Item #T170x-2020

Using Technical Analysis
Clifford Pistolese

Technical Analysis for everyone! Easy-to-understand primer
explains an array of approaches to analyzing stock market
charts: chart patterns, volume analysis, timing tactics, trends
and more.
$24.95 Item #T170x-3553

Prechter's Perspective
by Robert Prechter

Robert Prechter on the Elliott Wave Principle, Market Analysis
and the Nature of Social Trends. Timeless commentary "reveals
the full bounty of the Wave Principle" and shows how it relates
to investing and popular culture.
$19.00 Item #T170x-2543

The Visual Investor
by John Murphy

Track the ups and downs of stock prices by visually comparing
charts—instead of relying on complex formulas and technical
concepts. Introduces readers to Intermarket Analysis—a proven
analytical approach based on evaluating the impact different
markets have on each other. Includes software demo disks and
instructions for using charts and graphs.
$39.95 Item #T170x-2379

The Arms Index (Trin Index):
An Introduction to Volume Analysis
by Richard Arms, Jr.

Finally, it's updated and back in print! Get an in depth look at
how volume not time governs market price changes. Describes
the Arms' short term trading index (TRIN), a measure of the relative strength of the volume in relation to advancing stocks
against that of declines. Also shows how to use Arms' own system to forecast the price changes of individual issues as well as
market indexes. A true trading gem.
$39.95 Item #T170x-3130

Analyzing Bar Charts for Profit
by John Magee

A straightforward guide teaching the timetested approach of using technical analysis to minimize risk and boost profits. From the bar chart "king" you'll learn: Classical chart patterns; How to identify trends and trading ranges; Tops, bottoms and what they mean to your bottom line. Plus, the "Magee Method" of buying/selling. "It's the best explanation of the technical process ever written."
$39.95 Item #T170x-2318

Handbook Of Technical Analysis:
A comprehensive Guide to Analytical Methods, Trailing Systems and Technical Indicators
by Darrell Jobman

An in-depth look at all aspects of technical analysis. The roster of contributors is a "Who's Who" of trading: Wilder on RSI, Schwager on uses and abuses of technical analysis, Pring on momentum, Prechter on Elliott Wave and more. From bar charts to candlesticks, volume to Gann—it's a #1 guide to the profit-grabbing techniques of the masters.
$55.00 Item #T170x-3419

New Market Wizards
By Jack Schwager

Meet a new generation of market killers. These hot traders make millions—often in hours—and consistently outperform peers. They use vastly different methods, but share big successes. Now, you can meet them and learn their methods. How do they do it? How can you do it? Learn their winning ways with this bestseller.
$39.95 Item #T170x-2106

The Art of Short Selling
Kathryn F. Staley

Finally, a book showing how to cash in on this lucrative yet overlooked strategy. Staley explains what it is, how it works, best type of companies to short and never before released methods of the world's top short sellers. There's no better time to position yourself to profit from any stock sell off.
$49.95 Item #T170x-2006

Pattern Price & Time:
Using Gann Theory in Trading Systems
James Herczyk

Here's the first book to simplify Gann's breakthrough techniques for beating the markets. Also shows how to integrate Gann theory into modem computer charting methods.
$59.95 Item #T170x-8438

Profits in Volume:
Equivolume Charting
by Richard W. Arms, Jr.

This method places emphasis on trading range and volume considered the two primary factors in technical analysis. They give an accurate appraisal of the supply/demand factors that influence a stock. With this critical factor you can determine if a stock is moving with ease or difficulty and—thereby—make more on-target investing decisions.
$39.95 Item #T170x-6780

Point & Figure Charting
by Thomas J. Dorsey

Here's the first new work on Point & Figure in 30 years. Today's leading expert shows how to use point & figure to chart price movements on stocks, options, futures and mutual funds. Learn to interpret the point and figure charts and recognize patterns that signal outstanding opportunities. Also covers how to combine point and figure with technical analysis for unbeatable success. You can't afford to pass by this valuable trading tool, and Dorsey makes it easier than ever.
$59.95 Item #T170x-2364

Candlestick Charting Explained
by Gregory Morris

Brand new book on this phenomenal indicator takes the guess-work out of candlestick analysis. Go beyond the basic theory to build a thorough system using the latest in computer analysis techniques and to identify trends, patterns, tops, bottoms and more.
$35.00 Item #T170x-2347

Technical Analysis of the Financial Markets
By John Murphy

From how to read charts to understanding indicators and the crucial role of technical analysis in investing, you won't find a more thorough or up-to-date source. Revised and expanded for today's changing financial world, it applies to equities as well as the futures markets.
$70.00 Item #T170x-10239

INTERNET SITES

Traders' Library Bookstore
www.traderslibrary.com, the #1 source for trading and investment books, videos and related products.

Equis
www.equis.com, creators of MetaStock, the popular technical analysis software, this site offers a full range of powerful technical analysis tools for more profitable investing.

Bridge Financial
www.crbindex.com, a comprehensive source of products and services for futures and options traders. This "onestop" site offers current quotes, online data, books, software products, news and information from one of the world's leading financial information source.

Martin Pring IIER
www.pring.com, the only site dedicated to teaching the art of technical analysis and charting, from one of the most respected authorities in the industry.

Wall Street Directory
www.wsdinc.com, the best directory of financial sites on the web. A comprehensive source that will help you find the answers to all your financial questions, and point you in the right direction.

Dorsey Wright

www.dorseywright.com, the top source for information on Point & Figure analysis and comprehensive Point & Figure charts.

Equity Analytics

www.eanalytics.com, an excellent educational resource with extensive glossaries for technical analysis and many other topics.

FutureSource

www.futuresource.com, a comprehensive source of information for futures and other traders providing futures quotes, settlement prices, charts, FWN news, chat rooms and other useful tools for traders of all levels.

Murphy Morris

www.murphymorris.com, the site of Technical Analysis gurus John Murphy and Greg Morris. A perfect site for both beginners and those more experienced in Technical Analysis.

Track Data

www.tdc.com, a supplier of electronically delivered financial data since 1981 with several services specifically designed to assist day traders. Timely market data, financial databases, historical information, data manipulation tools and analytical services are available.

Bloomberg

www.bloomberg.com, this major financial web site has it all: news, quotes, hot market information, lifestyle updates, investing tools and resources, research—and more. Turn to the industry leader for all your financial needs.

MAGAZINES

Technical Analysis of Stocks and Commodities
www.Traders.com, an industry leader in providing current, cutting-edge articles, interviews and product information for traders, with a significant focus on technical trading. This well-known monthly publication also features a special bonus issue each year, and regularly rates and awards the industry's top software products and other technical analysis tools.

Individual Investor magazine
www.individualinvestor.com, is the fastest growing investment magazine in the country, carving out a unique niche by addressing the needs of the growing ranks of individual investors. Readers get specific recommendations about specific stocks and mutual funds, plus information in industries to watch, winning investment strategies, international investing, and more. The "Magic 25" list of top picks has finished with cumulative returns over 200% over the past five years.

Traders World magazine
www.tradersworld.com, covers trading stocks, options, and commodities with winning methods and technical analysis from top experts in the field. You'll find classical tactics and methods of masters such as W.D. Gann and Elliott Wave—plus sophisticated new state-of-the-art computer techniques used by today's top traders.

Futures Magazine

www.futuresmag.com, filled with information for futures and options traders, plus books, videos and dates of their popular trading conferences.

NEWSLETTERS SPECIALIZING IN TECHNICAL ANALYSIS

The Dines Report
Editor, Jim Dines
P.O. Box 22
Belvedere, CA 94920
800-84-lucky
$179/24 issues

Dow Theory Letters
Editor, Richard Russell
P.O. Box 1759
La Jolla, CA 92038
619-454-1265
$233/36 issues

The Elliot Wave Theorist
Editor, Robert Prechter
P.O. Box 1618
Gainesville, GA 30503
770-536-0309
$233/12 issues

Inside Track
Editor, Eric S. Hadik
P.O. Box 225
Naperville, IL 60567
$179/12 issues

InvesTech

Editor, James Stack
2472 Birch Glen
Whitefish, MT 59937
406-862-7777
$250/18 issues

Leading Indicators

Editor, Clif Droke
816 Easely St., #411
Silver Spring, MD 20910
$144/50 issues

The Master Indicator

Editor, John T. Goddess
11371 Torchwood Court
Wellington, FL 33414
$100/24 issues

P.Q. Wall Forecast

Editor, P.Q. Wall
P.O. Box 15558
New Orleans, LA 70175
$198/12 issues

The Reaper

Editor, R.E. McMaster
P.O. Box 84901
Phoenix, AZ 85071
830-598-8255
$195/36 issues

Stockmarket Cycles

Editor, Peter Eliades
P.O. Box 6873
Santa Rosa, CA 95406-0873
707-597-8444
$480/18 issues

The Wellington Letter

Editor, Bert Dohmen
1132 Bishop St
Suite 1500
Honolulu, HI 96813
800-992-9989
$265/9 months

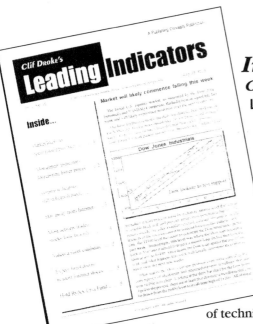

Introducing

Clif Droke's ...

LEADING INDICATORS newsletter

Discover **Leading Indicators**—the industry's top technical advisory service. This hard hitting, weekly publication covers the U.S. and global equities and commodities markets from a technical perspective. Each and every week you get thorough—*timely*—coverage of all major stock indices, as well as precious metals markets—using a wide array of technical tools including...

- Basic technical analysis
- Elliott Wave Theory analysis
- Japanese Candlestick analysis
- Dow Theory analysis

Plus, comprehensive analysis and forecasts of the market's near-term and intermediate-term direction—EVERY week, 50 profit-packed issues per year.

Order a no-risk subscription—TODAY!

▪ ▪

Cliff Droke's LEADING INDICATORS
Only $144 for 1 year (50 issues)

☐ Yes, enter my subscription for 50 weekly issues of *Leading Indicators* for just $144. I understand that if *Leading Indicators* ever ceases to be profitable reading, I may cancel my subscription and receive a credit or refund on all remaining issues—no questions asked.

☐ Payment enclosed   Send check or money order for $144 U.S.
(Sorry, no credit card orders) to:
Leading Indicators, 816 Easely St., #411
Silver Spring, MD 20910

Name & Title: _____

Company: _____

Address: _____

City: _____ State & Zip:_____

About the Author

Clif Droke is a popular technical analyst, newsletter editor and author. He is the editor of *Leading Indicators* newsletter, a weekly publication covering U.S. equities markets and socio-cultural trends from a technical perspective. He is also the editor of other newsletters, including Clif Droke's Internet Stock Outlook and the Gold Strategies Review. For these investment and trading publications, he analyzes several major sectors of the U.S. and global equities markets using the principles he outlines in Technical Analysis Simplified.

Mr. Droke is also the author of the book *Elliott Wave Simplified*, which *Technical Analysis of Stocks and Commodities* magazine says, "teaches investors how to apply these simple and proven methods to the stock market."

NOTES

NOTES

NOTES

NOTES

NOTES

NOTES